THE PRESIDENCY OF THE 1970's

THE PRESIDENCY OF THE 1970's

Proceedings of the 1971 Montauk
Symposium on the Office of the President
of the United States

Sponsored by:
CENTER FOR THE STUDY OF THE PRESIDENCY
Proceedings: Volume II, Number 1, 1972

iii

R. GORDON HOXIE
Editor

Contributors:

James M. Beggs
Harvie Branscomb
Daniel E. Brennan
Mary S. Calderone
William J. Casey
Ray B. Chambers
Robert H. Connery
Brutus Coste
Luther H. Evans
Thomas W. Evans
James H. Finch, Jr.
Benjamin Frank
William M. Franklin
C. Edwin Gilmour
Robert N. Ginsburgh
Joseph A. Grimes, Jr.
James C. Hagerty
David Haight
E. S. Harris
Martin S. Hayden

Abraham Holtzman
Blahoslav Hrubý
Dwight A. Ink, Jr.
W. Maxey Jarman
Gary Kugler
Edward C. Lyon
H. F. Mackensen
Harvey C. Mansfield
Glen W. Martin
H. Coleman McGinnis
Joseph P. McMurray
Henry Paolucci
Robert A. Podesta
John R. Price, Jr.
George E. Reedy, Jr.
Helmut Sonnenfeldt
W. Clement Stone
Richard A. Ware
A. J. Wann
John A. Wells

Preface

In the period since April 1970, when the Center for the Study of the Presidency held its first national symposium at Montauk, profound changes have occurred in American life and in our relations with other peoples throughout the world. Since then this Center has conducted many lectures, round tables and symposia in points as diverse as El Paso, Texas, New York City, and Warrenton, Virginia.

Volume I, 1971 of the Center's *Proceedings* had been based upon that first Montauk Symposium. It was entitled, *The White House: Organization and Operations.* Its publication had been prompted by the observation of Dr. Dwight Waldo, Editor-in-Chief, *Public Administration Review,* when he wrote: "This certainly appears to have been a well planned symposium on a topic of utmost importance. I am sure that political science, and particularly public administration, will benefit from the publication. . . ."

In selecting what should comprise Volume II, the Center's Board of Editors called upon the joint criteria of historic importance and relevancy. In so doing it chose one of two additional symposia which have subsequently been held at Montauk, that of October 29-31, 1971, participated in by 175 business, governmental, and professional leaders from throughout the nation. Again, they were in the pleasant setting of Gurney's Inn, a salubrious site, long a favorite of the President, 120 miles out to sea, near the Eastern tip of Long Island. Again, far from being down on the beaches, they were in sessions from early to late, seeking to present, by historical, present, and projective analysis, *The Presidency of the 1970's.* Here then for the first time are published the discussions of 41 of the conferees.

The round tables were primarily participated in by governmental leaders past (serving with Presidents F. D. Roosevelt, Truman, Eisenhower, Kennedy and Johnson) and present. Additionally there were college presidents, editors, lawyers, historians, librarians, and political scientists, who held their own, weight-wise, far more than one of the governmental group, former Presidential Press Secretary, George E. Reedy, Jr., was willing in the discussions to give credit. But the academicians have since had their revenge, since Mr. Reedy has succumbed to becoming one of them, as Dean of Journalism at Marquette University!

Although the academicians dominated the questions herein raised, the cogent observations of national business leaders, like W. Maxey Jarman of Genesco, and of attorneys, like John A. Wells, of Royall, Koegel, and Wells, added a further dimension to this printed record. In many ways perhaps the most haunting question was raised by an academician who is a Federal servant, Dr. William M. Franklin, Director of the Historical Office, Department of State. Looking back over 30 years with the Department he could observe: "At the end of World War II the prestige of the United States was unchallenged. The historian," he added, "may well ask how in the past 25 years has that prestige diminished. Was it lost in summit meetings or was it lost in the national will? . . . What brought our travail of the 60's?"

Dr. Franklin re-echoed the sentiments of other participants, including Under Secretary of Transportation James M. Beggs and President of the Academy of Political Science, Dr. Robert H. Connery, when he emphasized that "before seeking to plot any new courses for the 70's we might well reflect upon the national purpose, the national determination." Like so many other of the participants, Dr. Franklin further affirms that "if some of this can be regained in the 1970's, less force would be necessary for American leadership to be effective throughout the world."

It was only when posed with the unrelenting questioning of internationally famous director of Sex Information Education Council U.S., Dr. Mary S. Calderone, that the all-male round tables faltered. But then youthful Special Assistant to the President, John Roy Price, Jr., rose to the occasion. He recalled when an even younger Abraham Lincoln, as a member of the Illinois legislature, responded to such an embarrassing question by diving through an open window. Fortunately, in this instance no one did to the ocean far below. Instead, the chairman called upon an American safety valve, the coffee break.

Here then is a volume which this Board of Educators deem a worthy sequel to *The White House: Organization and Operations*. So many of the domestic and foreign policy issues raised in that earlier volume find definition or resolution in this. Decision-making, relationships with the Congress, and governmental reorganization appear with increased clarity with the passage of time from that early April 1970 symposium to this more than 18 months later at the end of October 1971. It was a time in which the first Nixon Administration was reaching its maturity.

As National Security Council Senior Staff Member, Helmut Sonnenfeldt expressed it, "The key issue that this Presidency . . . has had to confront is the change in the power balance and power structure. . . ." The ending of America's clear nuclear superiority by the mid 1960's simultaneous with its engagement in what was to become our most controversial and protracted war, had been complicated by the emergence of five power blocs, i.e. China, Japan, and Western Europe, in addition to the Soviet Union and the United States. It had further been complicated by mounting trade imbalances and inflation placing strains on the American dollar both abroad and at home, civil strife, and unrest which by 1968 had placed the American Presidency under great stress.

In this volume one views the responses to the pressures domestic and overseas, the pronouncement that the New Deal is dead, that a New Federalism and renewed individual responsibility would be coupled with revenue sharing and decentralization of authority, along with the consolidation of Cabinet Departments.

Here then are examined these changes at home and abroad. Light is perceived at the end of the long tunnel in Vietnam and new relationships with mainland China and the Soviet Union come into view. To give additional currentness to our strategic posture, the subsequent remarks of Lt. General Glen W. Martin, Vice Commander in Chief, Strategic Air Command, were added here with the approval of the Department of Defense.

Further pointing up the wisdom of the soldier-scholar and his concern for domestic as well as foreign affairs issues is the observation of Major General Robert N. Ginsburgh, then Chief, Office of Air Force History, now Director of Information, Office of the Secretary of the Air Force. ". . . the major foreign policy problem for the 70's," General Ginsburgh asserts, ". . . is to cope with the foreign policy issues in a way that will enable us to devote the time and energy we will need to devote to some very key domestic issues."

Chairman of the Securities and Exchange Commission, William J. Casey, perceived the relationship between the domestic and international economy, the national will and foreign policy. ". . . where we stand and how we perform as a nation in international competition," Mr. Casey emphasized, "will have a great deal to do with the kind of living standards and the kind of economic health we enjoy." By such an observation, Mr. Casey, a founder of this Center, was then unconsciously setting a challenge for his own role in the second Nixon Administration as Under Secretary of State for Economic Affairs.

In concluding this preface we should be remiss not to speak of our special gratitude to two persons. The one is the Center's able editorial associate, Miss Sheila Halpin, whose promise as a history graduate student at City University of New York joined with her skills acquired at Katharine Gibbs, finds fulfillment in a myriad of editorial chores, including those related to this volume. The other is again our host at Gurney's, that remarkable Keeper of the Inn, Mr. Nick Monte. The President will appreciate our remembering Mr. Monte, and the pleasant memories on the brink o' the beach.

This Center found inspiration for its founding in the person of former President Dwight D. Eisenhower, who wrote of the Center concept shortly before his death, "The result cannot fail to be good . . . for the nation."

The Center staff found particular encouragement from former President Lyndon Baines Johnson, whose health precluded his participation in the 1972 National Student Symposium (also held at Montauk). In expressing his regret, Mr. Johnson wrote, "The work you are doing for the Center for the Study of the Presidency interests me very much. . . ."

In a meeting at the Center on January 26, 1973, four days following Mr. Johnson's death, the co-chairmen for the 1973 National Student Symposium, which will have as its theme the title of this volume, proposed an appropriate dedication to Mr. Johnson. And so to him and to the principles of human dignity for which he stood, this volume is respectfully dedicated.

In an irony of history the initialling of the cease-fire agreement for Vietnam had occurred the day following Mr. Johnson's death. As President Nixon stated in announcing the agreement, "Just yesterday a great American who occupied this office died. In his life President Johnson endured the vilification of those who sought to portray him as a man of war. But there was nothing he cared about more deeply than achieving a lasting peace in the world. . . . No one would have welcomed this peace more than he."

And so this preface is completed as America, the world, enter upon new relationships. As President Nixon expressed it, "We must recognize that ending the war is only the first step toward building the peace." As Dr. Kissinger expressed it in a January 24, 1973 news conference, "no one in this war has had a monopoly of anguish . . . no one . . . has had a monopoly of moral insight." As this volume suggests, Dr. Kissinger concludes that as we join in "healing the wounds in Indochina we can begin to heal the wounds in America."

In this program of reconstruction for a peaceful Asia, a peaceful world, Mr. James Reston concludes in the *New York Times* on February 23, 1973 that "Mr. Nixon is now clearly embarked on the most constructive American enterprise abroad since the Marshall Plan in Europe after World War II."

Just a year, almost to the day, after the President's historic journey to Peking, announcement was made of the beginning of the normalization of relations between China and the United States. In this volume we discuss the then proposed summitry both with Peking and Moscow. As Secretary of State Rogers declared in a statement before the House Foreign Affairs Committee on February 8, 1973: "Looking back, we can see how important those initiatives were in giving substance to the concept of dialogue in international affairs."

Also in this volume we discuss what is termed the Nixon Doctrine. A portion of that, enunciated in July 1971, focuses on economic policy. It suggests the international economic challenges we face in the balance of the 70's, there being now not two or three but five super economic blocs: China, Japan, the Soviet Union, Western Europe, and the United States.

With severe trade imbalances still persisting, with the dollar devalued twice in 14 months, we face an uncertain economic future. As the President expressed it in his February 22, 1973 State-of-the-Union Message, "the state of our union depends fundamentally on the state of our economy." He concludes with the warning of President Franklin Roosevelt, that "we could be 'wrecked on (the) rocks of loose fiscal policy.' " Here, then, in the economic sphere, as we seek to help build peace and stability at home and abroad, may well be found the greatest challenge to the Presidency of the 1970's and to the American people.

For the Board of Editors
Kenneth W. Colegrove
Luther H. Evans
R. Gordon Hoxie
John O. H. Stigall
New York City, February 24, 1973.

Foreword

by

W. CLEMENT STONE, *Honorary Chairman*
CENTER FOR THE STUDY OF THE PRESIDENCY

The American Presidency is a *human* institution. In their overriding concern for organization and powers, this concept escapes many students of the Presidency. Such was not the case, however, in the 67th Annual Meeting of the American Political Science Association in Chicago. There on September 10, 1971 Dr. Hoxie traced the origins of the Center for the Study of the Presidency. He read from the statement, written shortly before his death, of the late President Eisenhower, under whom Dr. Hoxie had served at Columbia University.

Mr. Eisenhower emphasized this humane approach to the study of the Presidency. He pointed up the importance of an "accurate picture of an individual's capacities, qualities and character." He expressed the hope of "an appreciation in each case of the responsibilities carried, the mutually conflicting considerations prevailing, and the tensions of the particular time. . . ."

Favorably impressed by this approach to the study of the American Presidency which has characterized this Center, at that Chicago meeting I accepted Dr. Hoxie's invitation to participate in this Montauk meeting.

It is a special privilege to join with you in this Symposium devoted to an examination of the American Presidency in the '70's. Each of us participating in these discussions can follow through with some programs that will prove beneficial to the Nation. In our discussion of the United States Presidency in the 1970's we must think not only in terms of the office, but also in terms of the experience, ability, habits, and philosophy of the President. For it is the leadership in a corporation, country or any institution that determines the course it will take by virtue of the power its leaders hold.

To better understand the domestic and international problems and to develop successful solutions to them, it is imperative that we throw the spotlight on those who hold high public office—their passions, tendencies, emotions, instincts, feelings, moods, and habits. For when we deal with the progress, problems and activities of a nation, we are dealing with people. It is in this joint approach, studying both the institutions and the people who serve in them, that I commend to you the reading of the record of this Symposium.

I for one feel strongly that it is the *use of the power* of his office by the President or Chief Executive of a country, corporation or institution that determines the course it will take. And it is the character, ability, attitude and experience of the Vice President, or the individual who would replace the President in an emergency, that determines whether that course is likely to be followed.

We have been and are living in an age of conflict in which our inherited basic political philosophies and our personal, moral and ethical standards have been and are being attacked.

We are at a very important crossroad which will determine whether we shall pass on to posterity our Constitutional freedoms inherited under the American free enterprise system or . . . whether we shall take a submissive, socialistic course that will deprive our children and their descendants of a government based on a political philosophy that has made us the greatest nation on earth. Let's therefore seriously consider the American Presidency in the '70's.

The Presidency is a position of power. As the national leader of his people, the President is in a position more than any one person to direct the course of the future of our nation. He can use the power of his office to prevent the recurrence of many of the difficulties we have experienced in the past at home and in other parts of the world.

We are off to a good start: the Vietnamization Program has proved to be a successful basic principle whereby we can help free nations defend themselves in the future against aggressors rather than by sacrificing American lives as we have in the past . . . a potential catastrophic inflationary trend is being neutralized . . . the transition from a war to a peace time economy is being experienced in an effective manner and . . . personal, direct communications and meetings with leaders of foreign governments by our President have brought about understandings that indicate the possibility of a generation of peace among nations.

The Presidents of the '70's will be key figures . . . perhaps the most important world figures as to whether or not the people of the world will learn to live in peace. If we are to live in peace, the President must have the courage to keep our nation militarily strong . . . strong enough to discourage a war with us by a potential enemy.

Military strength will be necessary until the leaders of our potential enemies, by their actions as well as their words, indicate a sincere desire for peace. To bring about this desire for peace by them, there must of necessity be good-faith communications between our leaders and those representing foreign nations.

The channels of commerce with China, Russia and other Communist states are now being opened that can add to the prosperity of the United States and raise the standard of living of the peoples of these nations.

President Nixon has said, "What kind of nation will we be? What kind of world will we live in? Whether we shape the future in the image of our hopes is ours to determine by our actions and our choices." And . . . "Let us not fall into the dreary rut of just managing the chaos a little better . . . let us use the great power of this place (the Presidency) to do something for the nation." Mr. Nixon also said, ". . . the real problems we face are not scientific nor technological but ethical in nature."

Let us at this Symposium concerning the American Presidency in the '70's try to share ideas that will in some way help shape the future of America by the actions which we shall initiate here that could make America and other nations in this world better places in which to live for this and future generations.

Table of Contents

THE PRESIDENCY OF THE 1970's

CHAPTER I

Dialogue on the Changing Presidency

A. *Introduction by R. GORDON HOXIE*

Good evening, ladies and gentlemen. Welcome to Gurney's Inn and our Second National Leadership Symposium on the Presidency. In the first National Leadership Symposium we sought to broadly portray "White House Organization and Operations." Our topic this year is "The Presidency of the 1970's."

As so many political scientists have observed, the sponsoring Center for the Study of the Presidency and this symposium both have qualities of uniqueness in focus and resources in approaching the major issues of our time, as well as in dealing historically with the Presidential Office. Our richest resources are in our membership and in our participants, as represented here this evening, who have a common concern and meeting ground in strengthening our basic nongovernmental and governmental institutions. Emphasizing both our historical and projective approach, we have with us this evening both distinguished historians participating in our national bicentennial projects and student chairmen for our next National Student Symposium.

Perhaps our Center's most precious heritage is the conceptual view given us by the late President Eisenhower, who had proposed the establishment of a Center devoted to Presidential studies, placing search for truth above partisan considerations.

Several of the members of our Board of Educators and of our National Advisory Council are here. As one of the members of both, Dr. Harvey Branscomb, Chancellor Emeritus of Vanderbilt, expressed, we should in this Symposium examine "both some of the broad policy issues and some of the specifics." In doing so we shall review the changing American Presidency from the early 1930's to the present. We shall both philosophically and pragmatically examine some of the issues of our time. We shall seek to project domestic policy for the 70's, followed by a similar projection on foreign policy. We shall conclude Sunday morning by focussing on how the Presidential Office should be organized for the future in order to best implement policy.

The Hoover Presidency makes a good beginning point. It

marks the transition from the old Presidency to the new. It was Mr. Hoover who initiated the Presidential task forces which we associate with the modern Presidency in the formulation of policy. Most notable was the series of recommendations emanating from President Hoover's Research Committee on Social Trends, headed by Professor Wesley C. Mitchell of Columbia University. From this came much of the philosophy and economic and social legislation of the ensuing New Deal Period. It was also from Mr. Hoover that the Reconstruction Finance Corporation was born, bringing government into closer relationship with business.

There followed in the growth of the modern Presidency, the record 12 years of service in peace and war of F. D. Roosevelt followed by the eight years of peace and war under the remarkable Harry S. Truman. Our focus this evening will be on the Presidency beginning with Eisenhower, and we examine the years in a bi-partisan spirit.

We begin this evening then with an especial examination of the changing American Presidency of the 1952-72 period. Our two uniquely qualified examiners were both testifying yesterday before Senator Birch E. Bayh Jr.'s sub-committee on constitutional amendments. They were asked: "Should a President be elected for only one six-year term?" What are the implications of such a question? Does it suggest the title of a recent book by one of this evening's speakers: *The Twilight of the Presidency?* Does it suggest a challenge to our institutions; a change in our sense of purpose; an interruption in the pursuit of the goals which were enunciated by our Founding Fathers in the 1775-1789 period; or a breakdown of the machinery they established to help achieve those goals? Are we by Constitutional amendment or by the will of the people moving inevitably toward one-term Presidents? These, in turn, are some of the questions which I hope these two gentlemen will seek to answer.

Recently, both President Nixon and former President Johnson have expressed, in writing, their interest in the work of this Center, pointing up our bi-partisan character. The fact is that both former and present Cabinet members and national chairmen from both major national parties are represented in Center membership. I see in the back of the room this evening one of those former chairmen, Leonard W. Hall. As Professor Matthew

Holden, Jr. of the University of Wisconsin put it: "If you can claim the support of both James A. Farley and Leonard W. Hall, of both G. Mennan Williams and W. Clement Stone, then your Center must be as close to unique as anything will get in this world."

Our two speakers this evening represent this bi-partisanship. One is a distinguished life-long member of the Democratic Party, and the other a distinguished life-long member of the Republican Party. Both are perceptive students of the Presidency. Neither needs an introduction. Both were chosen unanimously by the Student Co-chairmen who heard them in our first student symposium. Both served as Presidential Press Secretaries, Mr. James C. Hagerty with President Eisenhower, and Mr. George E. Reedy, Jr. with President Johnson. First, let me call upon Mr. Hagerty, a member of this Center's Board of Trustees and Vice-President for Corporate Relations of the American Broadcasting Company.

B. *The Presidency of the 1950's*

JAMES C. HAGERTY: Ladies and gentlemen, while I am a Republican, when I talk about the Office of the President, I think you will find that I talk apolitically. For the eight years I was there, and since then, I have formed a healthy respect, admiration, and empathy for the man who occupies that big White House on Pennsylvania Avenue. The late Merriman Smith, who was for many years the dean of White House correspondents, used to say that the President was a man of many things; that is exactly what he is in our modern Presidency, which I would date really from Franklin Roosevelt's days.

Let me just first run over what I think are the basic responsibilities and duties of the office that really do not change very much over the years, although the emphasis on problems change, of course, from term to term, and from decade to decade. The American people, and the people throughout the world, expect our President to be a man of many things. For example, he is the Chief Executive of the largest corporation in the world—the Federal Executive Department, with its farflung activities not only in our country, but throughout the world. His decisions affect not only the lives of all of us in this country but also the lives of many of the other peoples of this world.

3

By Constitutional assignment, he is also Commander in Chief of our military forces, and he, and he alone, has to make the awesome decisions in regard to our military actions. Sitting on his shoulders from the second he lowers his hand in taking the oath of office, is the horrendous arsenal of nuclear weapons. He has to be a man of great wisdom and great patience to bear that burden.

He is also, or should be, the diplomatic leader of the Free World. He has to try to get along with our friends and allies, no matter how difficult, at times, those friends and allies may be. He has to try to get along with the neutral and the developing nations. He has to try to open up new peaceful lines of communication with those nations of a different ideological approach from our own. And, he has to deal, particularly in these days, with dissent at home on the conduct of foreign affairs.

He also is, or should be, the leader of our nation in setting the moral and spiritual tone of our country. He has to strengthen, defend, and preserve the basic Constitutional principle that in our form of government all men are created free and equal, that they have an equal opportunity for gainful employment. At the same time, he has also to see that the laws in our country are preserved so that we can continue to be a progressive society.

He is also the acknowledged political leader of one of our two major parties; as such he has to play hard, tough politics to gain his point of view and to rally public support. In so doing, he is automatically aware that he will have his policies dissected and opposed by members of the opposition party and dissenting members of his own party. But he also has, in the political sense, to forego partisan politics and do what he thinks is in the best interest of our country. And this I think he does quite often.

He is also the leader in what we call in Washington "the hospitality brigade." He is sought by executive secretaries of every organization one can think of, for countless breakfasts, dinners, meetings, what-have-you, most of which are a complete and utter waste of his valuable time.

Finally, he is the sole, authoritative spokesman of his administration, and as such, his statements are dissected and magnified by the governments of this world, by the peoples of our country, by the Congress, and certainly by the news media—all of whom may have conflicting points of view on what he is trying to say.

Now this is what a President has to do. It is a multiplicity of jobs, but I think that each and every President handles it quite well in his own way.

Now, coming specifically to the President that I had the great honor and privilege of serving, President Eisenhower, I have argued with many people that you cannot compare Presidents unless you compare the decades in which they served. In my book, the '50's were a great deal different from the '60's and the '60's were a great deal different from the '70's.

Mr. Eisenhower was elected President only seven years after World War II. When he came into office, he inherited a foreign war, Korea—to be sure, a UN war and not a unilateral war. But the time was such that he was able to send word through the Indian Government to North Korea, to Peking, and to Moscow, that if they did not settle the war, there would be no imaginary line across the Yalu River. There would instead be hot pursuit of their planes regardless of where they came from. They happened to believe him, and they sat down to talk.

This was a lot different situation from what the present President inherited, and a lot different from what Mr. Johnson inherited. Remember, when Mr. Eisenhower came into office, we had military superiority; at that time we also had nuclear superiority. It was an entirely different world and an entirely different ball game.

I have a very healthy respect for our military establishment, which is much maligned at the present time. I don't know anyone who has been through a war who wants to go through another one! Mr. Eisenhower was one of those who did not. On more than one occasion, Leonard Hall, who is with us this evening, heard him say, as I did: "There is no such thing as a little force—don't ever use it. If you have to use force, use it in overwhelming superiority and get it over with fast." Now he only did this once as President. That was in Lebanon where President Camille Chamoun asked for American assistance. In those days, in 1958, Mr. Eisenhower sent 25,000 Marines and airborne infantry. That was the end of the trouble in Lebanon.

Again, it was a different decade. Mr. Eisenhower came into office following service as Supreme Commander in Europe in World War II and Supreme Commander NATO, with a resulting personal knowledge and acquaintanceship with the leaders of Europe and most of the leaders of the rest of the world. Many of the problems that arose in the 50's were settled by personal phone calls between the President of the U.S. and the leaders of other countries.

In addition, I have always thought that the Russians had a great deal of respect for him. In 1954 I was at Geneva, at the Geneva Conference, at his villa one evening. As the Head of State always does, he had the Russians in for dinner. There was N. A. Bulganin, Chairman of the Council of Ministers of the U.S.S.R. He was ostensibly the head of the delegation. In actuality, N.S. Khrushchev, then a member of the Presidium, descended from the car first; thus we assumed Khrushchev was the real head. There was also the Defense Minister, Marshal G. K. Zhukov, and the Foreign Minister, V. M. Molotov. On our side, there was our Secretary of State, John Foster Dulles, and three or four others. In our conversations with the Russians that evening, we really could feel a mutual respect for each other—not necessarily agreement, but a mutual respect.

So, in the field of foreign affairs, I feel Mr. Eisenhower had a built-in respect. Again, I am talking about the 50's and not the 60's, and 70's.

In the field of domestic affairs, it was a period of national prosperity. Our states were relatively solvent, and surprisingly enough in the 50's, so were our cities. The most crucial civil rights confrontation in the 50's was Little Rock, in 1957, a tea party compared to Watts, Newark, and other confrontations of the following decade.

The same was true with our young people. I think that Mr. Eisenhower really had the overwhelming support of the younger people of our nation. Ecology was a word used by professors—no one else knew anything about it—in the 50's.

We have heard that Mr. Eisenhower was not a political leader nor a politician. Still, historians now agree that his eight years of office look better and better as you look back on them. I think he was one of the best politicians I have seen in operation. He had one basic understanding that is fundamental in politics. He had mastered the art of compromise, of achieving the common good without the surrender of principle and of integrity.

This was certainly true in his relationships with the Congress, a Congress that was controlled by the opposition party for the last six years of his Office.

The leaders of those Congresses were two of his personal friends. Speaker Samuel Rayburn in the House, and Senator Lyndon B. Johnson in the Senate. There were days after days of meetings with Mr. Rayburn and Mr. Johnson, where if the President needed support on a Bill, they would say: "Mr. President, we'll get you those votes." And they did. Or they said: "Mr. President, you haven't a chance of getting those votes,"—and he did not get them.

Yes, he could work with the leaders of the Congress on the opposite side, probably as well as any man we've had in the White House.

I agree 50% with my friend George Reedy on his views set forth in his book, *The Twilight of the Presidency*. I do not think that the Presidency is getting to be an impossible, unmanageable job. But I do agree that we are in danger of having a cycle of one-term presidents where the "outs" outpromise the "ins" and when they get into the White House, can't deliver. I think the danger is that we may be in one of those cycles. Both George and I have just come from testifying our opposition to a proposed Constitutional amendment which would limit the Presidency to one six-year term. A President should have the opportunity to run on his record. The danger is the lack of understanding of that record. That is one reason why I view the work of the Center for the Study of the Presidency as important.

Perhaps, the best way to end these remarks is to read you a letter that Mr. Eisenhower sent me. It is dated October, 18th, 1966. It says:

Dear Jim: Attached is a list herewith, by no means complete. A few days ago, I was asked for a list of accomplishments of the Republican administration. [I think it is quite interesting that he did not say *my* administration]. I dashed these off from the top of my head along with a few comments. I thought you might be interested [which was the understatement of the letter]. It seems that the deportment and words rather than the achievements of people in the position of heavy responsibility are taken by columnists and partisans, and at times, by serious students, as evidence of the true capacities of those of whom they write. They equate an individual's strength of dedication with oratorical bombast; determination, with public repetition of a catchy phrase; achievement, with the exaggerated use of the vertical pronoun. They ignore completely the circumstances that have made difficult any progress by any of their victims; just as they do the accidents and planned publicity that often made easy the way of the exhibitionist. To them record means little. Manner and method are vital. Yet, consider these accomplishments:

1. The statehood of Alaska and Hawaii;
2. Building the Saint Lawrence Seaway;
3. End of Korean War (Thereafter no American killed in combat);
4. Largest reduction of taxes to that time;
5. First civil rights laws in 80 years;
6. Prevention of Communist efforts to dominate Iran, Guatemala, Lebanon, Formosa, and South Vietnam;
7. Reorganization of the Defense Department;
8. Initiation and great progress in the most ambitious road program by any nation in all history;
9. Slowing up, and practical elimination of inflation;
10. Initiation of a space program which successfully orbited within three years, after starting from scratch;
11. Initiating a strong ballistic missile program;
12. Conceiving and building the Polaris program, with ships operating at sea, within a single administration;
13. Starting federal medical care for the aged (the Kerr—Mills bill);
14. Desegregation in Washington, D. C. and the Armed Forces without laws;
15. Fighting for responsible fiscal and financial policies throughout eight years;
16. Extension of old age insurance coverage to over 10 million persons;
17. Intelligent application of federal aid to education;
18. Preservation, for the first time in American history, of adequate military establishment after the cessation of war;
19. Using federal power to enforce orders of a federal court with no loss of life;
20. Goodwill journeys to more than a score of nations in Europe, Asia, South Africa, and the Pacific.
21. Establishment of the Department of Health, Education, and Welfare;
22. Initiation of plans for social progress in Latin America after obtaining necessary authorization from the Congress;
23. Atoms for Peace Proposal.

All of this was done with the Congress controlled by the opposition party for six years, the other two having only a nominal Republican majority.

I think that letter speaks for itself. I will end on that note. Thank you very much.

GORDON HOXIE: Well, thank you very much James Hagerty, for that succinct statement; assuredly it was an historic one, including the words of the late President Eisenhower. It was, as I indicated in my introductory remarks, a similar expression of concern for understanding of the Presidency "by serious students," which inspired the founding of this Center.

Let us turn then to that other good friend of the Center who has expressed such interest in our programs, George Reedy, student of the Presidency, [soon to be named Dean of Journalism at Marquette University].

C. *The Presidency of The 1960's*

GEORGE E. REEDY, Jr: Thank you, Gordon. Jim put his finger on something extremely important. I think the reason that Jim only agrees with me fifty percent of the time is that Jim's close contact with the White House was in the 50's; mine was in the 60's. As Jim said, the decade of the 60's was quite a different thing from the decade of the 50's.

The decade of the 60's, I believe, was the era in which the institution of the Presidency was brought to its sharpest challenge. There were always strains inherent in the office; flaws which were inevitable as there are flaws in all human institutions. But strains and flaws began to appear in the early 60's which led us into a terribly troublesome era. I am still standing by the opinion that was expressed by the title of my book. I do not think that we are out of the woods yet.

To present this concept to you clearly, I have to start with a certain academic distinction which may at first seem to be mere quibbling. When you apply it to the actuality through which we have all lived in the last 12 years, however, I think you will see that it is an absolutely vital distinction.

We all speak of the Office of the Presidency as having the "power." To fully understand that office, or any other political office, you have to realize that there is no power whatsoever in any political office. A political office is an institution which we set up and designate as a legitimate instrument through which political power can be exercised.

The power of the Office of the President is the political power that a President brings into it. The power is not in the office but in the political relationships of the man who holds the office with his people. You may note that this is true of any political position or any government.

This becomes important because anytime in a nation when

9

you reach a stage where the sole instrumentality through which power can be exercised suddenly loses that power, the nation undergoes very heavy strains. I think that this is what happened to us in the 60's, and it has happened before in our history. If you examine the history of the United States prior to the Civil War, you will find that we had a series of Presidencies which were very similar to the recent ones—one-term Presidents, unable to take action. There was, for example, James Buchanan, who did not stir, and who has been blamed by history for not moving when the South began to secede from the Union.

In retrospect I have a great deal of sympathy for that man because I suspect that he was very much in the position that Lyndon Johnson was at the end of his Administration; that Harry Truman was in toward the end of his; and that Herbert Hoover was in at the end of his. The truth is that he did not move, because he could not move. He did not have the political power.

I really think that the trends which led to this appeared before the 60's. I will go along with Jim Hageity; I will be more generous than he; I will agree with him 100 percent on the statements that he made that Eisenhower was a master politician. I did not think so at the time. I was a typical, partisan Democrat. The list that Jim read to you of the accomplishments of the Eisenhower Administration, is the same list that Lyndon Johnson would read at the end of every session as the Democratic accomplishments, as he was in charge of the Congress which passed those bills. We were playing our own games too. I had, what I now realize was a somewhat naive idea that this man was a "pushover." We believed that we were the master politicians—that Eisenhower did not really know what he was doing and that we were the geniuses that were guiding the developments. Lord, it is funny how different things look a few years later.

I really believe today that he was a master politician, and that the two Eisenhower Administrations postponed the showdown that we had in the 60's. Eisenhower recognized, possibly instinctively, possibly consciously, some of the stirrings through which we were going, and he conducted himself masterfully so as to bring this country some tranquility and some serenity, and to forestall some of the conflicts we began to have again in the 60's.

During the late 40's and 50's, the Truman-Eisenhower period, this was, as Jim Hagerty has indicated, a nation of many assets. We had nuclear superiority, we had military superiority, and the country was solvent economically.

Mr. Truman is one of the men I admire more than almost any other political figure that I have known. There are very few others that stand on a par with him as far as I am concerned. He had courage, he had fortitude, he had goodwill, and he had "guts." But in that last year in office (1952) he did not have one thing—he did not have political support. As a result the country reached a stalemate in which government became a question of minimum housekeeping in which only the bare, minor essentials were attended to.

One of the most vivid memories of my life was serving on the staff of the special committee set up under Senator Richard B. Russell to conduct the hearings on the Far East. These were actually the hearings on General Douglas MacArthur's return. When those hearings started out, Senators Richard Russell, Lyndon Johnson, and Brian McMahon, and I were all really deeply concerned on how far the divisions in the country would carry—just what was going to happen. People were standing out in the streets with tears in their eyes, greeting a returning General as a proud hero, and booing and hissing the man who represented the legitimate power of the country. I still think to this day that Richard Russell, one of the most underestimated men in American political history in my judgement, really saved this country.

We had a similar period in that last (1932) year of Herbert Hoover. I was very young then, but once again I think differently in retrospect. There was a man of integrity, a man of intelligence, and a man of goodwill, but a man of no political power. During his last year, the country was hopeless. Hoover did not have the kind of relationship that enabled him to inspire the American people and get the country moving again.

When I re-examine F. D. Roosevelt's programs, I am not as sure now as I was then, that it was the intrinsic merit of them that saved the day as much as the confidence that was behind them—basically the good will of the people. In short, if a President has enough political strength and enough of a following among people, his programs will work even if they are drawn up by 12 inspirations for idiot children. If he does not have that kind of strength, and if he does not have that kind of enthusiasm, his programs are not going to work even if they are drawn up by the finest minds we can assemble.

In essence, this is the basis of the Presidency, and this is why we make such a mistake when we denigrate politics. The Presidency is a political job. The President is the political leader of the country. He is a man who must inspire people, who must make programs work, even if they are bad programs; who must give the people a sense of unity, a sense of participation in the country; and who must make them feel proud to march under its banner.

If we turn now to the 60's we can see this syndrome in operation once again. President Kennedy, in my judgment, was definitely losing his political force at the time he made his tragic trip to Dallas. In fact, the reason he went down there is because Texas, which was a key state, was falling to pieces politically.

President Johnson's entry into office engendered a tremendous wave of enthusiasm. I believe that the American people were grateful to him for the continuity that he gave; for the feeling of reassurance that there was still a strong hand at the rudder. Three or four years later he could not go out in the streets without being booed and hissed.

I do not think we have worked our way out of that syndrome yet. There are a number of reasons for it. The obvious, immediate one is the Vietnam War. Whether it was right or wrong (and history is going to have to take a very long view of that) it was still not a war that the American people understood. It was not a war which inspired them. They woke up one morning and found their sons were fighting in some country far away that they had never even heard of. This caused part of the breakdown. I think another thing that it did was to exacerbate the whole increasing trend of democratic government away from the people in an age where face-to-face contact with the Presidency is no longer a possibility. That does not mean that in the past every American citizen had face-to-face contact, but it is amazing how many did. I am fascinated in reading Carl Sandburg, to discover that even during the Civil War, ordinary citizens could walk off the streets and into the White House and have a conversation with Abraham Lincoln. That could happen in those days, and apparently that rule held for a considerable long period of time.

Very few Americans, obviously could meet the President face-to-face, but it did not particularly matter because, before Franklin D. Roosevelt, government to most Americans was not a question of the Presidency. They only heard about the President every four years during the big campaign which was a form of entertainment for them.

The real government, to the average American, consisted of his mayor, if he were a big city type like me, or his alderman. If he were a rural type, it might consist of the county sheriff or the county judge, or the local Congressman. These were people he did know face-to-face; these were people that he could meet.

In the early 20's, when I was a small boy, even if you were a poor Irish immigrant or a poor Italian immigrant, you still had a voice reaching into City Hall on a rather honest, face-to-face basis. You would have a precinct captain who would come around at Thanksgiving with a turkey, and, maybe, at Christmas with a half-ton of coal, and it was all an open, above-board transaction. It was dignified. All he wanted was your vote. You did not have to fill out a form explaining how many children you had; or if you used contraceptives. You did not have to stand there with some cold-eyed Social Service worker looking you in the face and testify as to whether you had a wife or an old maid aunt; or whether you had a man hidden in the cellar who didn't have a job. People believed that the precinct captain who gave you the coal, and to whom you in turn gave your vote, was their government.

With Roosevelt, of course, began the age of "mass government." Two forces began to work against each other. One was that people suddenly became highly conscious of the President; the other was that the President, as they became more and more conscious of him, became more and more an aloof figure. As time went on, the President gathered more and more power unto himself. I believe this was essential. I am not one of those people who think you are going to run this country without considerably more power in the Executive—even more than there is today.

Our problem is not keeping power away from the President, but finding some way of *humanizing* this power so that once again we will have a political leader who is part of our people and who can understand the lives and times under which most of us live. He would still have to face adversary comment and adversary fighting as all the rest of us do. I think we have to bring the Presidency back to a human basis.

I agree fully with Jim on this question of a series of one-term presidents. I believe that it is going to happen. Some of them may have two terms, but it's going to be an accident if they do. It is going to be because the opposition party has fallen down on the job, or because some temporary concatenation of circumstances really prevents the American people from kicking the rascal out. I think they are all going to be considered "rascals," until once again we establish some kind of consensus in this country; until once again we find some kind of forms which will take the President out of the mass, impersonal age and restores the incumbent to the position he must hold above all others, as the political leader of the people, as the man who inspires us and who holds us together and the man who keeps us in unity.

CHAPTER II

Security, Diplomacy, Freedom of Information, and Scholarship

GORDON HOXIE: *Introduction*

We have entitled this First Roundtable, "Security, Diplomacy, Freedom of Information, and Scholarship." The gentlemen who are seated here on the podium this morning in a very real sense represent each and all of these concerns. Our moderator is James C. Hagerty, who, along with George E. Reedy, Jr., who is seated at his left, presented our keynotes of last evening. On my right is Dr. William M. Franklin, who heads the U.S. Department of State's Historical Office with great distinction. When we were in the process of seeking goals and objectives for the new Center for the Study of the Presidency, he was one of the first people that I went to. Accompanying me was another member of this panel, Dr. Luther H. Evans, the chairman of our Board of Educators at the Center for the Study of the Presidency, the former Librarian of Congress, and the former head of UNESCO. Like Dr. Franklin, he is not only concerned historically with these matters, but also very much currently.

Also on the panel this morning is one of America's most distinguished editors, Martin Shaw Hayden. A son of a great journalist, and a graduate of the University of Michigan, he began as a young cub reporter in Kansas City, Missouri. He came on to Detroit in 1930. He was a political editor in his early years, and as a foreign reporter, he covered a number of the major international conferences including Geneva in 1954 and the Berlin Foreign Minister Conference ten years later. He is today the Editor-in-chief, as he has been since 1958, of the *Detroit News*.

Also with us is the distinguished Chancellor Emeritus of Vanderbilt University, member of our Board of Educators, and member of the National Advisory Council of our Center, Dr. Harvey Branscomb.

Mr. Hagerty, the floor is yours as we begin our session: "Security, Diplomacy, Freedom of Information, and Scholarship."

JAMES HAGERTY: The titles Dr. Hoxie has picked for this first roundtable: "Security, Diplomacy, Freedom of Information, and Scholarship," could be discussed for three or four years, and we would still not be quite finished with the subjects! Let me as moderator turn first to George Reedy for his comments on these topics.

GEORGE REEDY: The thing is so big, I am not sure where to take the can opener and get it opened up. Looking at the combination of considerations, there has been one trend over the past 40 or 50 years which I do find of some concern. It is an extremely difficult problem, and I believe that it is going to cause a lot of head scratching and a lot of soul searching—the matter of security.

Security, to begin with, involves the security of the United States—not only the physical aspects of security, that the Armed Forces deal with—but also the question of secrecy,—of classified information, and of diplomacy. Diplomats are men who, often for good reasons, but frequently just because it is a habit they have become accustomed to, like to conduct their negotiations in great privacy. On the other hand, the next topic is "Freedom of Information" which is absolutely essential to any democratic society.

We have here what is normally considered a dichotomy. We believe that, on the one hand there is a certain value, the freedom of information, and on the other, there is another value which centers around security and deep privacy. Within our Government itself, there are secrets which have to be withheld and negotiations which have to be conducted quietly. We assume that in one instance this *Right* shall prevail, and in another instance the opposing *Right* shall prevail.

It is, however, an unfortunate mistake to suppose that the two are absolute values, exclusive of one another. What really exists here is a situation in which there are two sides to the coin, as there are to all coins. Even when there is an absolute need for security and for classification, you still have to pay a rather heavy price for it.

Let me illustrate. In looking at the Pentagon Papers, which I have studied fairly carefully, I am not at all convinced that they shed any light on history whatsoever. There is no real way of knowing which of the papers reached the President and which did not, and in the Federal Government if a paper doesn't reach the President, it does not mean a thing. If anything, the papers will probably confuse history because of the lack of sure knowledge as to which of those things had an impact and which did not. I am also thoroughly convinced that their publication was a service, but it would have been far better had they been published back in 1964 and 1965 when they were being written.

Why? Because no matter what we think about the Vietnam War, the point is that the American people one day woke up and found themselves in a conflict that they had no idea was coming and in a far, remote corner of the world that few even knew existed. Their sons were being killed; there was a drain on the Treasury with all the dislocations it has had on the economy and in our political structure. I think the rising tide of opposition which eventually forced some type of withdrawal came more from the fact that the people thought they had been sold a bill of goods than it did from actual considered judgment toward the war itself.

The only debate that went on about our entry into that war was within the Government itself and within relatively few parts of the Government. Historically, when this nation has entered a war, the move has been preceded by a rather large debate. By the time we entered World War II, almost every American felt he had had his say, almost every viewpoint had been expressed, and I think we initiated our part in that war with a sense of unity and of purpose.

Points of view had been expressed by this time, and some of them quite passionately. I can still recall the mob that hanged Senator Claude Pepper in effigy in the Capitol Plaza across the streets from the building. There were the "Mothers of America" storming down to Washington and the Sons and Daughters of "I will Arise" sitting down in the Senate Office Building corridors and that type of thing. It was a very turbulent scene which everyone thought was subversive. In retrospect, I do not think it was subversive, because I do not think the disunity over the war would have vanished if we had not had that stormy and turbulent decade.

I think one of our problems with Vietnam today is that disunity arose from the fact that we did not have a genuine national debate and could not, under the security system that has arisen over the last 40 years.

This is not a plea for the abolition of security. Anyone who believes that many affairs of the world, and certainly our defense posture, can be conducted under a magnifying glass is just being somewhat naive. I do think that in this question of security, we have made the mistake of withholding from the American people the basic elements of national debate and that without debate you cannot rally the people to support of the very difficult policies that a country must undertake when it is at war.

For that reason I am rather glad to see this question of Freedom of Information tied to Security and Diplomacy. Here you have one of the fundamental elements of the problem. If you are going to withhold the basic factors of debate, then you are going to have the very great problem of trying to mobilize the force behind our policies. I'll just throw that one out for whatever discussion you have.

JAMES HAGERTY: Thank you, George. My own personal experience in eight years is that we have a rather archaic system within our Government. Actual security is necessary. The United States in dealing with its friends and allies around the world and in discussions with foreign nations has to maintain security.

But we have a number of people who sit in front of their desks with a pile of security stamps on them. At about the third or fourth echelon, someone puts "Confidential," on a paper. It goes up to the next echelon and that person says "Well, why did the fellow in the fourth echelon put "Confidential" on it? Maybe I better put a "Secret" on it." Then the Cabinet officer who is going to send it over to the White House decides that to get any attention, it should at least be marked "Top Secret," or "For Eyes only," or believe it or not, "Burn Before Reading!"

There were many times in the eight years that I was in the White House that I would get papers from various departments that I was going to release at my next press conference. But if they had security classifications on them, I had to go to get the President of the United States to initial the papers, thus declassifying them, so I could make it public. The only thing about those papers that will remain classified is what he was saying to me when he was initialing them!

The press in Washington should be a hairshirt for the Government. It should probe, and try not only to report what happens but how and why. It should continually analyze the workings of the Government.

But there are problems. For example, at the present time there are 125 million pages which are still classified from World War II. Twenty million of those pages are jointly classified by the United States and the United Kingdom. From Korea there are 50 million pages. The interesting observation has been made that with a five man committee going over these two sets of papers, it would take 458 man years to declassify them! The only really good solution is a good bonfire!

This leads me to our next panel member—an old friend of mine, one of the best Washington correspondents I ever knew. We had our arguments, but at the same time we also worked on a professional basis and after working hours we were close friends. During working hours I guess I was the legitimate enemy, but that is the way you work professionally in Washington.

It is a great pleasure for me that Martin Hayden is here. Martin, I turn the discussion over to you for whatever you want to say.

MARTIN S. HAYDEN: Thank you, Jim. We did know each other when we were earning our living in an honest way. I am sorry that Robert Semple has not shown up yet, because I am sure he would challenge me.

In an editorial, we (the *Detroit News*) took the position that we felt there was an irresponsibility on the part of the *New York Times* in not at least making an effort to get the Pentagon Papers declassified once they had them. I have a feeling if Scotty Reston had asked to see the President, had gotten to see him, and said "We have these and we want to know what is in this that you say is secret and has to be classified," there probably would have been a declassification. And, if not, if they then published, they would have at least, I think, gone into court with cleaner hands.

What worries me is this constant battle between the press and the bureaucracy to get information out. Of course, the information does get out with the result that the American people in my opinion, are the best informed electorate in the world and in history.

Too much is classified. This classification goes from the absurdity of a secret stamp being put on a post exchange fraud

19

in Europe to the manifest necessity of a design for a Polaris submarine being secret—and there is a gray ground in the middle.

But we have this amorphous system, and it works. Very few things that are secret stay secret in Washington indefinitely. The routine secrets leak. They are leaked by press secretaries when it serves the purposes of their bosses. They are leaked by members of the Congress who may be on the other side when it serves the purposes of their boss.

Take the Pentagon Papers. As you go through them, there is very little in them we did not already know. For instance, one great revelation was that President Kennedy had sent Green Berets into North Vietnam. Well, there was a novel written about that. It was a revelation, allegedly, that President Kennedy had supported the overthrow of President Ngo Dinh Diem and his chief political advisor, his brother Ngo Dinh Nhu. It's true it was the first time you had seen it in official writing, but certainly everyone who had read a metropolitan newspaper had not only known it was the case, but had also read Madame Nhu's accusation that the President was responsible for the death of her husband and her brother-in-law. These things were not secret. The people in general did know about them. They knew we had troops in Laos; they knew we had troops in Cambodia, despite the fact that the Government went through the charade of pretending it wasn't true. Now, however, the times have turned the spotlight on the *Times* case, on this gray area.

As you read the various opinions of the Supreme Court you discover that three Justices came out against the *Times* and then a clear majority of the rest said they could not rule with the Government because of the lack of legislation. Justice Thurgood Marshall made the specific point that the Court could not act when Congress had refused to legislate in this area.

What frightens me is that the next revelation of secret papers may not be well received. In the case of the Pentagon Papers the public was overwhelmingly against the Vietnam War, so they thought it was fine. But suppose tomorrow some officer in the State Department, who perhaps is somewhat anti-Semitic, decided that he should prevent a war and deliver to some editor, who perhaps is somewhat pro-Arab, all communications between Golda Meir and Richard Nixon and all the negotiations that are currently going on in the Middle East. I think the publication of such material would start a backlash the other way. Congress would then set out to straighten out the matter, and we would get an official Secrecy Act which would prevent anyone from releasing and publishing secret material under penalty of jail—as they do in England where they also have a considerable tradition of free press.

It also seems to me that we are seeing the rebirth of another "Hang the Kaiser" movement in this country, with a mass of people who think that someone has to be blamed for the Vietnam War. It reminds me of the McCarthy era two decades ago when the Senator from Wisconsin very successfully propounded the idea that our loss of China to the Reds had to be the fault of those who had been, or were, traitors in our diplomatic or military services during WW II.

Now we have the reincarnation of this period in a sense with Dr. Daniel Ellsberg as the Man on the White Horse, taking McCarthy's place and seriously propounding in *Look Magazine*, that there should be some sort of Nuremberg Trial, and all those that were in command or staff position in Government, military, or civil, should be banned from any further participation in government for the next 10 to 20 years.

This is the sort of thing that is totally destructive to the democratic system. Democracy can't work if people, when they are called upon by their superior, or by the President, for a report or advice, are going to have to say "Now what is going to happen if this thing leaks out in the future and it turns out to be wrong?" Of course you will have the safety factor working and they will tell the President nothing. In essence, you will have collapse of free government. I am afraid that the Pentagon Papers have opened up an area in which the press can be damaged and from which could come an official secrecy act which could destroy the present system which makes the American people the best informed of any on earth.

JAMES HAGERTY: Thank you, Martin. The Pentagon Papers, as you know, were prepared by the Department of Defense without the knowledge of the Department of State, which is inconceivable to me. It also published, with those papers a certain amount of contingency planning by our military. Contingency planning for future possibilities is absolutely essential as is its appropriate security classification. Most of the Washington press fully understand this. There were many times during my eight years there when a newsman had something that was true, but if published would seriously embarrass the Government. They did not use it. So newsmen have an understanding of the relationship between the Government and the press. The only things that make them get up on their high horse, and rightly so, is when they are told, "You cannot be told, you cannot investigate."

I agree with Mr. Hayden that there is a very deep danger that we could get some sort of secrecy legislation in the future, censorship if you wish to call it that. I do not think that it is going to happen but it could be tried, and it just might pass.

GEORGE REEDY: Well, I would like to take a somewhat different view on this. In terms of the contingency planning, in terms of the so called secrets in the Pentagon Papers, I am fully in accord with you that they do not throw much light on what happened. I think, in fact, that in the standpoint of history, we are entering a period where history as an intellectual discipline is going to become almost impossible. Historians will be so smothered under tons of paper, including the Pentagon Papers, that they are not going to have any clear idea as to which papers had relationships to what actually happened.

Then there is the matter of the national climate of opinion. I am thinking very specifically of the George W. Ball memorandum which was written in 1964 by the then Under Secretary of State and nothing that could be classified other than the fact that it revealed that there was a deep division in our Government.

There is one very important feature to our system of government and that is because we are not a parliamentary system, we do not get the type of adversary debate among leaders that you can get in other democratic countries. In the situation we had preceeding Vietnam and during the first few years of this war, the only sort of debate you had came from a Government that was speaking with a united voice, even though behind that voice there was a division. In that kind of a situation, you are not going to have national debate.

If you have the Assistant to the President for National Security Affairs sitting in a room with a college professor, the college professor is not going to carry much weight. If at that time, however, you had a government leader who could have been able to express his feelings publicly, I think that the American people would have had something to chew over. Thereafter, if we had, indeed, entered Vietnam whether or not it was a mistake, I believe we would have had a much more united country than we have today. I think that the disunity we have today flows from the fact that we took these gigantic steps without the public getting any kind of preparation at all for it. And this, to me, is the kind of danger you get into with this tremendous classification.

As to the other point of the dangers of a Secrecy Act, I really rather doubt it. You know that the Pentagon Papers were really unique. One of the factors that made it such a tremendous story was the sheer bulk of documents. You realize that as a rule, you do not have seven thousand pages all dumped into your lap. What usually happens, as a practical matter, is that all sorts of classified information comes out of Washington every day. It is almost impossible to pick up a paper that carries a Washington story in which there is not something that is secret or top secret. It just does not come out as a great big bulk or with a label on it saying "top secret." It usually is paraphrased in its release, and I believe that it will continue in that fashion.

JAMES HAGERTY: Now let us hear from the historians and scholars on this. You have heard from Martin, George, and myself. Dr. Franklin, what would you have to say on this?

WILLIAM M. FRANKLIN: When the Pentagon Papers hit the press, having been declassified in a somewhat informal manner by the *NY Times,* there was considerable consternation in the higher levels of government. There was an immediate self-examination to find out who does this declassification—who publishes this kind of paper—when and how? And why cannot we declassify as the *NY Times* did? Higher echelons looked around and down and eventually the finger pointed to the State Department's Historical Office, from which not much had been heard up to that point.

Yes, there is a procedure for declassifying even the top top-secret papers of the Department of State and publishing them. We, in the Historical Office, publish a series, which is ancient and honorable, called "Foreign Relations of the United States." The series began under Abraham Lincoln in 1861, as a series of documents annexed to the President's annual message to Congress. The papers were not just State Department papers. They were the President's showing the American Congress and people what our diplomatic correspondence and foreign policy had been in the preceeding year. Some of these papers of 1861 would have been marked Secret today, and we would keep them locked up for 15 or 20 years.

Times have changed; and, of course, no one much cared what we published in 1861 because of our isolation policies then and for many years thereafter. Mostly our ambassadors wrote interesting reports and our Department wrote back, saying "Stay out of all that." That kind of paper you can publish in a hurry. Anyhow, this series of volumes continued every year, and we are unique in having such an annual chronological series, which has now reached 1946—I wish I could say '56 or better '66.

In comparison with the foreign offices of other nations, our publication in the field of foreign relations is the most complete and the longest. Indeed, it is fully comparable to the Pentagon Papers in everything but time!

JAMES HAGERTY: Luther Evans. What would you like to say about this as former Librarian of Congress and a man who has spent most of his life working with it.

LUTHER H. EVANS: Mr. Chairman, I have spent most of my time fooling around with papers that are stamped "For Scholars Only." They are the kind of papers the *New York Times* would not print even if they had them. There are certain aspects that have not been mentioned that I think ought to be mentioned. As there are so many, however, I will mention only a few.

Libraries have considerable collections of private papers which are usually called Manuscript Collections, but those Collections frequently include material that originated in, or was directed to, the Government. The former Archivist of the United States ruled that a government paper, to be an archive, had to be one that had never left the Government's possession. As Librarian of Congress I was glad to know that, because the Library of Congress had many of these papers which had left the possession of the Government and had come into the Library's possession.

Such papers are in the hands of many libraries, usually with donor restrictions, and frequently with copyright restrictions—the so-called common law copyright. The common law copyright states that an author's works belong to himself and to his heirs and that no one can publish without the permission of the present owners. Congress is considering putting a time limit on the common law period of protection, but as of now you may note that George Washington's papers are still under that restriction, although no one observes it, as far as I know.

The revelation of these papers usually does not create any stir because they are old and they relate to events which are far beyond the possibility of hurting anyone at the present time. The problem here is one of access, and not one of the right to print, subject to the slight reservation which I have just made.

The main problem is that libraries frequently arrogate to themselves the right to control access. This means that they determine whether persons are using the papers for serious study or not and whether the person is qualified to do valid historical research. This also involves favoritism, particularly in the case of university libraries, so that some well-liked professor on campus will have first crack at writing the biography of Monroe or whoever it might be. This causes a great deal of irritation among the scholars, and rightly so. An equal amount of resentment occurs among the broadminded librarians who feel that if someone has control of important papers, they ought to be open to everyone to exploit at the same time and on equal terms.

Let me give you an example. Yale University, which is most uncooperative about letting non-Yale University professors use their choice Yale Manuscript Collections, has the original manuscript of De Tocqueville's *Democracy in America*. It shows enormous passages that he wrote and cut out. He wrote in a book and a series of bound notebooks. On the right hand side he wrote what he had to say, and then he crossed it out. On the left hand side of the page, he wrote the revision. There you can read (and I have read some of them) the passages which he scratched out, which, interestingly sometimes differed substantially from the passages he subsequently printed.

It is not right, in my opinion, for Yale to exercise constraints on the rights of everyone to have access to the De Tocqueville manuscript. As Librarian of Congress, I have fought for this sort of thing to be open.

There is one other aspect of this question which is important. Libraries that are collecting, frequently receive documents from thieves. One manuscript that the Library of Congress had at one time was a letter that Columbus had written. We bought it at an auction, or from a dealer, thinking that it was a copy. When we began to study it, however, we saw the stamp of the National Library of Spain on it. Somebody had overlooked that at the beginning. I wrote to Spain and said that we had it and would be glad to know whether it really had been in their possession. The Spanish government did not respond. It went to the newspapers, however, and they claimed that the Library of Congress had stolen the property of the Spanish Government. We called in the Spanish ambassador and gave him the letter to take home with him.

We have in the Library of Congress, a large proportion of the Colonial Archives of Peru. They were given to us by a donor who had obtained them from a book dealer, Dr. Rosenbach. The Peruvian Legislature, off and on, has a debate about the imperialism of these "Damn Yankees" who stole their archives. I decided that I should not return them, since this had been settled a long time before my period, but I did lay down the policy that we would not be involved in that sort of thing any more.

If anyone offers the Library stolen property, it will take it if it does not fall into this category. If, however, it is the cultural history of some country, it will not take it even as a gift. I think we ought to have an international treaty on that subject. Just recently UNESCO has drafted such a treaty covering not only archival material, but also various other kinds of cultural material. Many governments have recently tightened up regulations about the export of cultural property in their country. Great Britain is very advanced in this respect. If you go to an auction and purchase a portrait or other painting, or buy a manuscript book of the kind that they had in the Middle Ages, the British government will examine it to determine its importance to their cultural history before they will let you take it out of the country, even if you have already paid for it. In that case you are reimbursed and you go home without your property. I believe that in order to protect the cultural heritage of various countries, this type of restriction on scholarship must be approved. On the other hand we ought to put pressure on those countries to make the contents of this material available. They ought to allow microfilming of such papers without restrictions. I am hoping that UNESCO will do something in this field very soon.

Archibald MacLeish and I wrote a section in the UNESCO Constitution that the written and informational materials of all countries ought to be available to the peoples of other countries on the same basis as their own. We were not trying to eliminate security restrictions but rather to have the "open" materials open to the nationals of any country and all countries. This is more important to scholarship than it is for current use. I think that a lot of people have not drawn a clear enough distinction between freedom of access and freedom to print. They are two different conceptions and that ought to be kept in mind as well as what the First Amendment meant when it spoke of the freedom of the press and the freedom of speech. It meant that if you had access, you had freedom to print, but it had nothing to do, in my estimation, with the right of access.

Here, I feel that the *New York Times* may have been a little bit wrong in the case of the Pentagon Papers. They did not get the right to print, in my opinion, because they did not have the legal right of access.

There is another problem here that interests me and that is that certain information is given to the Government under the pledge of secrecy. We have all given information if we have ever filed an income tax return or filed a return for the U.S. Census. Now there is a threat to this secrecy if data banks are established including all the facts about a person's life, his arrest record, whether he was convicted or not, his census return, his tax returns, and many of his business transactions. If this kind of information is made available outside the Government, the contract is broken. Even if you leave out the secret government information covered by contract, you still have a trap for individuals because all of the information about them would be collected from many sources, would be coordinated, and conclusions would be drawn without clarifying the information itself. In brief, the computer, the data bank, could if misused, be a great threat to our liberties.

One area where we need great expansion of our informational control involves a scholarly problem and an administrative problem, rather than simply a problem of press and publication. This is the matter of environmental control. We need far more information in the hands of a great many more people about how much the water is polluted, and various kinds of air pollution; about the carbon content and the oxygen content of the air. We must have monitoring systems the world over, and we must have this information coordinated and distributed for purposes of environmental control.

UNESCO has been working on this subject, and has recently distributed a comprehensive report on procedures for such information dissemination. It involves national cooperation; it involves the cooperation of the scientists; it involves transmission of information between countries, whether their governments recognize each other or not, or whether they like the form of government or not. This is something that is being seriously worked upon by the librarians and scientists, and I suspect we will begin to see some important developments in this area, particularly regarding the Stockholm conference on environment which will take place next June.

Let me give you one more recent piece of information that is relevant to this issue. The *New York Times* got into the news in another way, a few years ago. It has a news sense, or it knows how to create news as well as to distribute it. It had one of its black reporters go into San Francisco and spend a year with the Black Panthers. This experience was followed by a series of stories about the Black Panthers. The local grand jury decided to investigate the Black Panthers on the basis of these stories and called in the reporter and asked him to testify. He was served a wide open subpoena. The *Times* resisted this, and the subpoena was narrowed to the point that he should not have to answer questions which violated his confidential relations with individual sources of news. He still would not appear.

It fell to me as a member of a subcommittee of the American Civil Liberties Union to draft the document justifying that position or at least determining what the position ought to be. We justified the position that he should not even appear before the grand jury, on the ground that this would jeopardize his sources of information. The Panthers, of course, would not know what had been said about them behind closed doors. We drafted this and had it adopted by the American Civil Liberties Union, and the U.S. Court of Appeals has upheld this. Newsmen under the doctrine of the law as it now stands, do not have to go before grand juries to report information which might jeopardize their sources of information through their appearance alone.

I am going to conclude now with a quotation from a conversation I had once with Eisenhower before he became President. I told him that I had been working on the problem of getting papers declassified, because the Library of Congress was very much interested in this, and I as a scholar was very much interested in it also. Ike admitted the point that many of the speakers have made here today, that there is excessive classification, and there is too little declassification. His words to me were "Keep working at it." Thank you very much.

JAMES HAGERTY: Dr. Branscomb, do you have anything that you would like to add?

HARVIE BRANSCOMB: I do not know why I am here, but I do like the environment. I have been very much impressed by the comments of Mr. Hagerty and Mr. Reedy both last night and this morning.

It seems to me that we ought to be thinking somewhat along a more positive line of which papers from the Government may or may not be published. Mr. Reedy has made the point, last night and this morning, of the lack of public involvement and the lack of public debate on these crucial issues. I would like to ask him and others on the panel a question:

In order to create more understanding of foreign policy issues, I believe more use could be made of the device of the so-called "White Paper." You probably would not get in the White Paper that balanced and objective presentation that scholars would like, but at least it would present to the rank and file of the public a discussion of the major issues of our country's policies. It would be of enormous help toward the understanding of the national course and in charting and delineating the national debate. This would have the value also, it seems to me, of reversing the psychology in channels of Government from that of restraining public access to instead encouraging constructive public communication.

I could not help but be intrigued by the figure that Mr. Hagerty mentioned of 50 million pages of classified material on the Korean War. I kept thinking about all the tens of thousands of graduate students who could be kept busy on M.A. thesis material and Ph.D. thesis material from these papers for the next ten years. This would release their preceptors for more serious business.

GEORGE REEDY: I think considerably more could be done, but unfortunately it still will not get to the heart of the problem. It is not so much a question of factual information because it is amazing how most of the things that really divide us and involve us in "gut-tearing" issues are not really disputes over facts.

Debate is essentially the presentation of *different points of view*. Partisans stand up and they argue, but the public has its best break when there is some kind of an adversary discussion and both sides are standing on the same level. Even though the Founding Fathers did what I regard as a superb job in establishing pluralism in our Government, the one area where the concept really breaks down, is the area that has been of the most vital concern to us for the last 20 or 30 years. That is the area of foreign policy and defense. In that there is no pluralism. You do not have adversary debators standing on the same level. What you do have, on the one side, is the President of the United States, the Secretary of State, the Secretary of Defense, and the Assistant to the President for National Security Affairs, all men that the American People quite rightly and properly regard as "The Responsible Officials." These are the men who bear the burdens, and who, therefore, should speak with greater authority. In most situations, that is right. I do not denigrate placing responsibility into the hands of these men, but we do have to give some serious attention *to the other side*. When you become involved in an adversary debate on matters of foreign policy and defense, the best you can have is maybe a college professor or maybe a speech made on the Senate floor or the House floor which will carry a little more weight than the words of a professor.

Consequently, this imbalance does not spark the kind of back and forth, hard, sharp exchange between men of different points of view needed for a good national debate. This is a relatively recent development. There was a time when you could get a very hard, sharp national debate going. I can still recall when Senator William Borah emerged from the White House after Roosevelt had called in the Congressional leaders to warn them of the danger that the War in Europe was imminent. Borah came out and announced very forcefully and very succinctly, that he had better information than Roosevelt did and that there was no possibility of a war in Europe. That particular statement was made in June of 1939. You may recall that the war broke out in September, 1939. The point is, that in that era you did have some means of stimulating adversary debate because the members of the Senate, particularly, could get an audience.

Over the years what has happened, however, is that foreign affairs and security have become so vital, and have assumed such a role (perhaps because we were involved in so many wars in such a short period) that today you really do not have a national debate. What you get is an authoritative statement from the Government itself, and this naturally carries weight. On the other hand, anyone debating the Government, looks as though he is some kind of nitpicker that is trying to elevate himself by becoming the adversary of great men. This to my mind, is the real danger, and is why I would have liked to have seen the Pentagon Papers published back in 1964, 1965, and 1966. I would like to have had the opportunity to read some of the George Ball memoranda in that period. The public would have regarded seriously these comments. I would have liked the public to have had some concept that within the Government, within that structure that they regard as authoritative, there were very real divisions. For that matter, I never heard George Ball speak the way he spoke in those memoranda in the National Security Council.

This is the type of thing that a White Paper cannot do because a White Paper is still going to speak the voice of the Government. In this matter, the voice of the Government is a united voice even though the debate going on inside the Government may be a raging thing. No word of this conflict leaks out. Therefore, the Government's position, which means the Administration position, comes down like a Sermon from the Mount. A White Paper cannot correct that, because it will still be the Government's White Paper. But how do you get this adversary debate? You can do it under a parliamentary system, and it is done under parliamentary systems, but I suspect that it is too late for us to go into a parliamentary system.

31

About the only thing that can develop is the occasional incident where a newspaper does take hold of something and publishes it in defiance. I hope, of course, that they will take the consequences of such an action if there are consequences to be taken. When I say that papers should be published, I do not say that the publishers are thereby exempt from the consequences. However, government should not prevent publication, which is a different thing. Mr. Evans made a very excellent distinction between the right of access and the right to publish. I think the right to publish has to be absolute. That does not mean that you cannot haul the person into court and into jail the next day, but I think he has to have the right to publish.

JAMES HAGERTY: Martin, do you want to add to that?

MARTIN HAYDEN: I just want to make a comment and pull a rather dirty trick on my friend George, by quoting from an excellent presentation last night by a man named Reedy. He pointed out that it was not the Office which had the right, but the President in it, and I would submit that if you had a touchy issue, free publication might inhibit discussion. George Ball, while Under Secretary of State, was not in agreement with the Secretary of Defense, Robert S. McNamara, and President Johnson on Vietnam. I wonder if the memoranda in question would ever have been written if he had thought it was going to be published the next week.

I do not think that you would have any adversary relationship within the President's administration unless it could remain confidential. It is true that Mr. Walter J. Hickel, while Secretary of the Interior, chose to publicly expound against President Nixon's policy, as a sort of "going-out-the-door" before it was slammed behind him. However, if a President is to get advice effectively from his Cabinet, that Cabinet member must have the courage of his convictions to state his position even though it is a minority position. Thereafter, he must remain silent publicly if his views are contrary to the President's decision. He says to himself: "Well, I did my best and now as a member of the President's administration, I will do the best I can to carry out his decisions." I really wonder if we would feed the national debate by publishing all debates within the Administration. I suspect that there would not be any debate at all within the Administration as a result.

GEORGE REEDY: Martin, let me make this point. First of all, it was publicly known that Ball was against the policy, but it was only known in a very general way when we were already in so deep that it was irrelevant. My point is not just to have it known that George Ball was against this. My point is that here was a rather convincing memorandum which marshalled a series of arguments that people could have chewed over and that would have sparked some thought. These were cogent arguments which I feel belonged in the public domain.

Secondly, I am quite aware of the fact that it is highly unlikely that he would have written those memoranda if he knew they would be published. As I said earlier, I am rather baffled about how you do go about stimulating that kind of adversary debate.

Thirdly, I am strongly of the belief that when newspapers do come into possession of material of this nature, they should publish it because I know of no other way of getting this out to the public. It is crude and it is raw, but I just do not know any other way of doing it.

I think the biggest single problem that we have today comes from the fact that we have stepped into some grave decisions and policies without allowing the public the kind of preparation that comes from really having chewed it over. I do not believe that our country can survive on the basis of a series of rude awakenings like the Vietnam War. I think you reach a point where the political necessity of mobilizing national support behind policies has to override the other considerations which normally seem sensible.

JAMES HAGERTY: Martin is right. Let me give you my feeling on this. Any President has to have people around him who have the courage to take the opposite point of view even if they themselves do not believe in it, just to make sure that the President hears all sides of the question.

The case that I recall the most vividly was that of Adlai E. Stevenson on a discussion of Vietnam. While serving as a member of the President's Cabinet under Kennedy and Johnson, he deliberately took the opposite point of view in Presidential conferences. He stated in *Look Magazine* that he did not always fundamentally believe what he was talking about when he presented the opposition case but he was making sure that his President was presented with all points of view. This happens in

Presidential circles and governmental circles all the time. This is what I think Martin is referring to.

Those discussions for the benefit of the top man in government, or the top man in a department have to be confidential. You have to present all points of view, even on the press side. You know, after all, you can argue with the President of the United States only up to the point when he says, "Thank you very much."

First Roundtable- Second Session

GORDON HOXIE: Before I give these written questions to Mr. Hagerty, I would just like to read a brief statement which has a certain Lincolnian philosophy about it. This is from a scholar whose presence here we welcome, *Dr. H. Coleman McGinnis:*

"The assertion that public debate is the most important factor in maintaining support for a policy seems a little stretched in terms of human nature. The American people will support a policy if it is working, given the fact that part of the problem is defining what success is. They will not support it, if it is not successful. There is a major difference here between what is best for *scholarship* [and a scholar has underlined that term] and what is best for policy making. What is most important, it seems to me, is to insure open debate within the councils of decision.

"No matter what proportion of the population supports the adoption of the policy, if the policy begins to fail, support will drop. Mr. Reedy would argue that the outcome, in large measure, determines how much support, in retrospect, a policy gets. If it fails, the great majority of people, even those that supported it, will be looking around for scapegoats, to "throw out" for failing to carry out their promises. In other words, policymaking is by necessity an elite function. People judge the results. Therefore, the most important point becomes the assurance of a full flow of information and debate within the halls of government." Signed Coleman McGinnis

MR. HAGERTY: Since that was addressed to Mr. Reedy, let Mr. Reedy answer that one.

GEORGE REEDY: I disagree with it totally and absolutely. Of course, people will always support success. Invariably people will support success even when the success is backed by some rather shoddy means. This is the whole history of humanity. Everybody likes to ride with a winner. The only difficulty is that I have never yet seen a policy that was such a complete success that people were going to ride with it.

I think the real basis of that question is that we probably have a disagreement over the nature of society and the nature of human institutions. I do not think there is anything like absolute knowledge that technicians can come through with or that can guarantee that policies are going to be successful or not successful. To say that a President should have access to all points of view within the Government, is to say that he should have access to his own point of view, because that is exactly what he is going to hear.

Early in the Presidential term there may be people who go up and give him the really heated, passionate adversary debate that he should have, but that is not going to last. Jim Hagerty also made the point that Presidents should have open to them all the divergent views of the people around them. That reminds me of an old, old saying: "If wishes were horses, beggars would ride." I also think that they should have access to divergent views. However, what I think we fail to realize is that a President is in an extremely unique position. He is one of the few men in the world who can really create his own immediate environment.

I will give you a very good example of the kind of adversary debate that I am thinking about. In 1954 when we were being pushed by Admiral Arthur W. Radford, then Chairman of the Joint Chiefs of Staff and the then Vice President Nixon to go into Vietnam to the aid of the French at Dien Bien Phu, Eisenhower asked Lyndon Johnson to sound out the sentiments of Senate Democrats for reactions. Johnson did this by calling a meeting of the Senate Democratic Policy Committee. I was present and that is one debate that I really wish I had a script of, because this was a passionate issue. There was fist pounding; there was yelling; there was screaming. Senator Walter F. George of Georgia, then chairman of the Foreign Relations Committee, was present to act as the Devil's Advocate and to advance the thesis that we should go into Vietnam. I will never forget the moment when Walter George said that we would lose face if we did not go into Dien Bien Phu. By contrast Senator Robert S. Kerr of Oklahoma, a big rugged oil man with a fist like a ham, slammed it on the table and allowed that he was more concerned about losing another part of his anatomy if we did go in. At the end of the debate, I believe, we had a really good human view of the thing.

A number of years later, I found myself sitting in such places as the Cabinet and the National Council, and everything was very gentle. I think when you reach the Cabinet you will find, for various reasons, that we usually appoint superior men to the Cabinet. I believe that in terms of caliber, you will find that they represent some of the highest levels of the Government. Usually the appointments are made right after an election, and a President wants to rid himself of all the implications of political infighting. They therefore usually reach out deliberately to find men who are distinguished in the real sense of the word.

But if you sit around the Cabinet you soon realize that everyone is very respectful and very quiet-voiced. You go around the table and finally reach George Ball. Everyone sits back and waits for the dissent which usually is something like; "Well, Mr. President, all I can say is where is this leading us?" That makes everybody very happy. They have heard both sides of the issue, and they go out and say that they have made up their minds after hearing both sides of the issue.

If you have a President who is effective, and who can lead the country, he is going to be a very strong and powerful man. In this particular syndrome, the stronger he is as a person, and probably the abler he is, the more likely he is to gradually lose the faces that are in there. They will not only stop coming in there with adverse facts, but they will even stop coming in with some of the moods and some of the passions. They will grow quieter and quieter. He will still have the technical facts presented to him, but again those technical facts are going to have a strange way of shaping themselves more and more to conform to the President's policies.

We have placed ourselves in a very dangerous syndrome in the modern age. We assume that because a series of facts are presented to us in a mathematical form, that those figures have given us an appearance of reality. I think it has reached such a point that I am looking forward to the time when in the liturgy instead of the Kyrie Eleison and the Apostle's Creed, somebody is going to stand up and recite quadratic equations or at least $E=mc^2$.

We forget that those figures are based upon assumptions. They can be very honest figures, and the assumptions can be honest also, but they are still based upon that. The technical advice coming into a President does not worry me because he is always going to obtain the type of technical information that he wants. We may, by some accident, someday elect to the office of President a combination of Aristotle, St. Francis of Assisi and Jim Farley, but it is a highly unlikely combination and I do not believe that you can base a government upon those happy circumstances. I also do not think that you can base a government on anything but the will of the people.

I do not understand this concept which seems so widely spread that there are a group of people transacting the people's business who have such superior knowledge that it is none of the people's business what they are transacting. I do not understand the belief that there are experts who know what the people should have, and therefore should have the right to proceed untrampled, without having the noisy, dirty, sweaty mob storming into their offices every day and without having to face all the unreasonable passions of our time. Passion can be handled. It can be handled, if you give the people a chance to get it out of their system.

You know that your foreign policy, as long as it is made by human beings, is not going to be all that successful. I do not care how much wisdom you bring into it or how much expertise you bring into it. About 50% of your policies, at best, are going to go sour. Maybe 25% of them will get you through reasonably well, and maybe you will have an occasional unalloyed success. However, you are not going to have the kind of foreign policy, as long as human error has a chance to play a part, that is going to be continually successful.

So—How do you hold a nation together? How do you make a government work unless you can guarantee policies that are so successful that people can recognize the results readily and will be willing to go along with the Government. If you do not reinstitute this question of national debate and let people blow off steam, no matter how unreasonably and how unreasoned, you are not going to have a country. You may have an extremely well-run country with some of the world's finest technicians; you may have people who have infinite knowledge and have the wisdom of all the ages; but you are not going to have a country.

JAMES HAGERTY: I have quite a few written questions here, and I will take some from the floor. If we are going to cover these questions, I would hope that the questions would be short and the answers would be short. I told you—I was bitten by Hubert Humphrey.

Martin, there are two questions which are somewhat related which are addressed to you. If I am unable to read the name of the individual who signed these questions, it means that their handwriting is worse than mine, which is saying something.

"Mr. Hayden, is there any possibility that the editors of the *Times* knew that, or at least surmised that during the 1964 campaign President Johnson was being secretly advised to expand American involvement in Vietnam? It is signed H. Mackensen. The second is from Professor Gary Kugler:

"Mr. Hayden, in addition to the inherent danger of a Public Secrecy Act, how would such an act affect the Senators' release of controversial and/or classified material such as Senator Mike Gravel's public reading of the Pentagon Papers?"

MARTIN HAYDEN: To take them in order, I think that the editors of the *New York Times* must have known about the advice to President Johnson if they had read their own newspapers. If you will think back, I do not think that anyone in the United States had any doubt that Barry Goldwater, when he was going through the country calling for defoliation and the like, was speaking the military line that was coming out of the Pentagon. I do not actually think that there was any plot or that Lyndon Johnson during the campaign was saying: "Wait till this is over, and then we will blow the hell out of them." As a matter of fact, the Pentagon Papers show that he was the one at this point who was dragging his feet.

On the matter of Senator Mike Gravel of Alaska publicly reading the Pentagon Papers, it has now come out in the *Look Magazine* article that Dr. Ellsberg went to Senator Fulbright, and various others and tried to give them the papers, and they would not take them. It certainly would have made a difference if Fulbright had taken them, and if Fulbright had put them into the *Congressional Record*. That would have meant an act by the Chairman of the Senate Foreign Relations Committee, and it would have been in the *Record*. Now, I am assuming that this would have been an Ellsberg-Fulbright deal, but apparently Ellsberg tried to make it that and Fulbright would not buy it.

As you know Ellsberg is very critical of Fulbright because of that refusal.

JAMES HAGERTY: Another question I have before me reads: "In his original foreign affairs account of his conversion on the Vietnam War, Clark Clifford said that during his first week as Secretary of Defense he reached an impasse by stating 'When I asked for a presentation of the plan for a military victory in Vietnam I was told there was no plan for victory in the historic American sense.' Would Mr. Reedy comment on why there has been no public debate on this extraordinary point that in early March, 1968, neither the President nor his Defense Secretary knew that there was a plan for a military victory in Vietnam?"

GEORGE REEDY: I think there was no public debate simply because it came after the fact. You know when you are talking about public debate, the public does not debate in the way that we do in high school or in a class on rhetoric. The public debates either what is happening to it at that very moment or what is going on which may make something happen to it. Again, the public really does very little debating about the past unless it has a direct relationship to the present.

JOHN A. WELLS: May I put this question to the entire panel, but particularly to Messrs. Reedy and Hagerty. I have been somewhat troubled with the practice which apparently sprang up first in the Franklin Roosevelt Administration and has been growing ever since, of writing history while you are making it at the White House. I am talking about such things as Robert Kennedy's book *Thirteen Days,* Goldman's book *The Tragedy of Lyndon Johnson,* and a lot of others. Then, of course, we have the *ex post facto* writings of President Eisenhower, President Johnson and so forth, about what happened historically while they were Presidents respectively. I think there are very serious ethical scholarship and security problems involved here, and I would like to ask whether the so-called Collection of Presidential Papers which are used to prepare the *ex post facto* publications are classified, declassified, or how they are handled.

GEORGE REEDY: First of all, I fully agree that history cannot be written in circumstances where people are right there on the spot. I have not even tried to and I am not going to. What I concentrate on is political analysis and political philosophy.

Second, I think there is a real service from Presidential Memoirs, not because they contribute directly to history but because they do give you something that you cannot find anywhere else, and that is how the Presidents saw themselves. That is a factor that history must take into account. Honest-to-God history cannot be written until decades after the event. The first decent historical book that I have seen on the origins of World War I, was Barbara Tuchman's *The Guns of August,* and that appeared more than forty years later.

The next point is that I think this tremendous documentation is going to hamper historians. When I think of the task of going through all the mountainous mass of papers that exist on Vietnam, and trying to make some sense out of them, I am appalled. It may be that history as an art, as an intellectual discipline, is going to disappear, unless we can devise some new techniques of selection of significant material. It used to be that only really important papers were saved because paper was expensive. Largely it was parchment, or sometimes papyrus. Today we save every little trivial thing that comes along.

In response to your last question on classification, I do happen to know a little about this, and Dr. Evans can probably correct me if I make a mistake. If there is a continuing classification on a paper in the Presidential library, it would still continue to have a classification. Over and above that, however, there are certain categories which are to be withheld from the public for a reasonable time period and I think under a reasonably accurate theory that publication of the papers at the moment might have an impact on some individual which would be unfair. If you go through these libraries, I think that you will find that some of the papers are to be released after ten years, and some after fifteen years. I do not know for certain what the outer limits are, but I think that it is 20 or 25 years.

JAMES HAGERTY: The only thing I would add, Jack, is that I think that the memoirs of a President, written by a President are his account of his administration and should be taken as such. But Mr. Kennedy was assassinated and those that wrote of the two and a half years of the Kennedy Administration were those that were pressured by the circumstances. These were staff officers or members of his administration and again, that is their account of what happened. As long as it is taken in the light that this is the opinion of the author, I do not think that we should be confused.

W. MAXEY JARMAN: Last evening it was mentioned that there were serious strains in our form of government. Last night you spoke of a lack of consensus of the American people regarding the status of the Chief Executive, and how this cycle might contribute to a cycle of one-term presidents. The question is: Would you say that a complete relaxation of the security restrictions by the government might restore public confidence in their government and therefore in the Presidential office itself?

JAMES HAGERTY: Let me try to answer part of this question first. I think that what I was talking about, and I am sure that what George was talking about last night, was not necessarily security and security restrictions. What we were talking about was the change in the decades between the 50's and 60's and into the 70's where the strain and the danger of this one-term president became a characteristic. 1972 is a whole new political ballgame. There are 27 million possible new voters. There are 11.5 million in the 18-21 age group. There are 12.5 million in the 21-24 age-group, who did not vote in the last election. Since the last Presidential election, the registration drive by minority groups throughout the country, has added 3 million more people. That makes 27 million. If you had given George, Martin, myself, or anyone else 100,000 votes in 1960 or 1968 and let us put them into key districts, we would have changed the outcomes of those elections. This is one of the strains.

The strain of foreign war by, in effect, unilateral United States action, rather than by multilateral action through the United Nations as in the case of Korea, has resulted in the lack of communication between the younger generation and those of my generation.

The problems of the cities, of the States, are all strains of the 1970's that are going to reflect, in my opinion, our selection of a President for some time to come. As I tried to say yesterday, my fear is that the "outs" will outpromise the "ins," and when they get in, find out that they cannot deliver. This is what I was referring to, and this is what I think, to a certain extent, George was.

41

GEORGE REEDY: I would add one thing to that, Jim. In describing the strains in our society, I would come up with about the same list. What has happened to us is that there is built into our system, as into any system, a degree of inflexibility. In the past, this has not been bothersome because most of the issues which affected us as a nation developed relatively slowly. There was time to adjust. It did not particularly matter if you had an unpopular President because everybody could wait four years. Nothing was going to happen that could not wait a few years more. It did break down on one occasion in our national history which was the Civil War. There we had a complete breakdown. In the closing months of the Buchanan Administration we had a man who could not even act to put down the open insurrection in some of the Confederate states.

What is happening now is that some of the inflexibilities in the system, which were not serious in the past, have suddenly become serious. They really did not become serious that suddenly, but we have suddenly become aware of them.

The principal inflexibility that I see, lies within the fixed term itself. When you put a man in office you have him in there, and he must stay, even when he has lost the political power which is so essential to govern. This is why I am so very strong in making this distinction between the office as the legitimate institution through which power is exercised. The ultimate power itself comes in many complicated forms. It may sound like I am saying something simple, but I am not. I am setting up categories, but within those categories, you are going to find many complexities. If you have that office, and the man in that office is incapable of acting under certain circumstances and there is no way of removing him, you really have some bad trouble. This is the principal reason why I am opposed to the six-year term. I think what it would do is to extend the tenure of ineffective Presidents from four to six. It seems to me that this is not a very good trade.

In the modern age where we do have these extremely rapid changes, and all the strains that Jim outlined, caused by even more fundamental problems in our society, we are beginning to really feel for the first time the impact of the fixed term. I think we have to live with it. As I was telling some friends out on the terrace, I do not believe that you can take some ideal form of government and say, "Boys, we are going to scrap our Constitution and we are going to start over with a new one." I am impressed by the fact that only two constitutions in the entire history of the world have proven themselves over a long period of time—ours and that of the British. I think they did because we started in a simple age, and evolved all the institutions that came along with them. Even now when these institutions are giving us a lot of trouble, I would not seek to change them fundamentally. What I would try to do is to find ways to become flexible within our system. These are the fundamental strains.

When I was speaking of the consensus, I was not speaking of the overwhelming consensus on the Presidency. I think the overwhelming majority of the American people still support the Presidency as an institution. The problem is that they have not found a man to put in it that really makes them want to "saddle up and ride to Jerusalem." When I speak of the consensus, what I am speaking of is the tremendous divisions within our country on issues. These divisions are so deep, and fragmented so much, that it is almost impossible to put into that office a man with genuine political power, because political power requires some consensus of opinion among the people. This is exactly what we do not have.

BENJAMIN FRANK: Since I managed President Nixon's campaign in New York State in 1968, I may be somewhat biased, but I would like to address two points to Mr. Reedy if I may, and take issue with two points that are open to discussion. One, you indicated as we talked about the Pentagon Papers, that unless a paper crosses a President's desk and he sees it, it is meaningless. I would take issue with that. I would say that policy papers and position papers that are directed to persons who influence the President in making his decisions have a great deal of meaning.

Jumping from that point, you have indicated, Mr. Reedy, that we had disunity that followed, after 1964, because of lack of discussion, and lack of debate. I submit that there was a great debate and that the debate took place during the campaign of 1964. I submit further that during a Presidential campaign, one has the attention of the American people and the opportunity for discussion, even in the hinterlands, more than at any other time. During the course of that debate, and during the course of that campaign, Barry Goldwater was pictured as a wild-eyed militant hawk, while President Johnson was pictured as a man of peace and a man of restraint.

Of course, Johnson said other things that certainly got lost in the newspapers, but this was the general impression that was left with the American people: Lyndon Johnson, man of peace; Barry Goldwater, man of war. Thereafter, following the campaign, the war was escalated at a tremendous pace. Bloodshed was now apparent for the first time, and at this point, the American people felt that they had been taken. This feeling of having been deceived led to the disunity, I submit, rather than did the lack of debate.

GEORGE REEDY: Let me take both of your points. First of all on the question of the papers that influence the President, essentially what you mentioned is an extension of that paper. I do not mean that the paper has to physically cross his desk; I mean that the substance of it has to physically reach the President even if someone carries it by word of mouth. The point that you have raised, however, illustrates my point that it is going to be even more difficult for historians because how are they going to know which of the papers reached somebody who was influential with the President? That merely makes the problem more difficult than whether the paper actually crossed his desk.

In regard to the second point, I really do not regard the 1964 campaign as having any real debate. In all due respect to Barry Goldwater, who is one of my closest friends and a man for whom I have a genuinely warm regard and affection, I never in my whole life in politics saw a man kick away votes as quickly as he did. I do not think he really wanted votes; I think he wanted converts. He did not want you to come to him unless you were "washed in the blood of the lamb." As far as his being pictured as a hawk, he pictured himself as a hawk. It is a strange sort of thing. I have never known a man who in his public image, which he created himself, is so completely different from the man himself. Barry Goldwater is a warm, kind, gentle man, I know of no one who dislikes Barry Goldwater that knows him. You cannot. He did it to himself in 1964. At that time, I think, he may have had a bit too much rhetoric. I am not going to go back into the past because I believe that Johnson believed everything that he said. I do not think that he wanted to get into that war.

GORDON HOXIE: On that historic note, since our time is up, may I express our thanks to Mr. Hagerty and to his distinguished, erudite panel in their broad ranging discussion of Security, Diplomacy, Freedom of Information, and Scholarship. It is clear from the questions of our members and guests that not all of the erudition is on this side of the table.

Earlier our Center Trustee, Jim Hagerty, concluded his remarks with a quotation from President Eisenhower. Let me now add another observation of President Eisenhower's, written shortly before his death, as to why there should be a Center of this character. He concluded, and I believe based upon this discussion you will agree: "The result cannot fail to be good . . . for the Nation."

CHAPTER III

Domestic Policies for the 1970's

Introduction by GORDON HOXIE

Following upon last evening's view of the changing American Presidency of the 1952-72 period, we turn our attention to domestic issues and policies for the 1970's. In doing so, we have an outstanding moderator and panel. Our moderator, Dr. C. Edwin Gilmour, Professor of Political Science at Grinnell College, combines the attributes of the scholar with a working knowledge of politics.

Professor Gilmour has campaigned for elective office and served in the legislature of the State of Iowa. Through the years, he has whetted the appetite of hundreds, indeed in a larger sense thousands, of students to meaningful careers of political service, and I shall ask him to first introduce one of those students.

C. EDWIN GILMOUR: Thank you, Gordon. Fortunately, for you and for me, my role as moderator of this session will be a minimal one. After brief remarks in which I shall attempt to place this particular conference session within the framework of the entire three-day symposium, I shall introduce the individual panel participants. Following the panel presentation, then, I will entertain questions from the audience and call upon appropriate panel members for response.

The proper and positive objective of the Center for the Study of the Presidency is to contribute—through research projects, professional seminars and public conferences such as this—to a better understanding of the constitutional session, the governmental and political roles, the public expectations and the behavioral realities of the institution of the American Presidency, as distinguished from the incumbents of this high office.

This afternoon, President Hoxie has assembled a most distinguished panel to direct the attention and thought of all of us to the topic of "The Domestic Policies of the 1970's." I make bold to offer a caveat to panel and audience alike. While our subject matter focus will be on current and developing domestic policies, we should employ the subject matter as an analytical matrix for the evaluation of both the strengths and weaknesses of the contemporary Presidency. Let us remember to center our observations and analysis on the personnel and procedures of the Office of the Presidency, rather than debate what our domestic policies are or should be. This evening's session, then, will pursue the same general objective, from the prospective of foreign, rather than domestic, policy formulation and execution.

The placing of these two sessions back-to-back represents good program planning. For the Presidency operates quite differently on the international forum than on the domestic scene. A recent study of the Presidency describes the powers, procedures, and problems of the Presidency relating to domestic problems, under the title "Prometheus Bound," suggesting that the President has too little power to meet the awesome demands made upon him by the American public. But the chapter reviewing the operation of the Presidency in the international sphere is entitled "Prometheus Unbound," arguing that the legal and political restraints on Presidential power to make and carry out foreign policy are inadequate and ineffective. I suggest that, in our discussions this afternoon, we attempt to identify and assess these constraints on the power of the President as he plays the central and critical role in domestic policy-making and problem solving.

The members of the panel for the session are all public servants who are serving—or who served—in one capacity or another, as a Presidential assistant. Each can speak from unique experience and confidence. More than this, all can assess the Presidency from different vantage points. For represented here today are three broad types of Presidential assistants, e.g. (1) the personal, albeit professional assistants in the Executive Office of the President; (2) the political appointee, of cabinet and sub-cabinet rank; and finally (3) those specialists who come into the executive branch on temporary assignments or as consultants.

And now to introduce the individual panel members. It is indeed a pleasure to present a former student of mine, now serving as an able member of the White House staff, John Roy Price, Jr., Special Assistant to the President. A native of New York City, reared on Long Island, graduate of the class of 1960 at Grinnell, he holds an M.A. from Oxford, where he was a Rhodes Scholar, and a law degree from Harvard University. Following graduation from Harvard Law School, he practiced in New York City and in 1967 was elected Vice President of the Bedford-Stuyvesant D&S Corp. A concerned student of urban affairs, he was appointed Executive Secretary to the Urban Affairs Council in the Nixon Administration. We at Grinnell are proud of him, and we are glad that he is now the Vice-Chairman of our College Board of Trustees. John, it is a pleasure to have you lead off, focussing on the major domestic policy issues of the 1970's.

JOHN R. PRICE, JR.: Thank you, Professor Gilmour, for that too generous introduction. What I would like to do is just to sketch briefly what I believe to be the principal issues of the 1970's in the area of domestic policy. I think it is now clear to everyone that one of the major issues emerging in the public discussion is the issue of our national growth itself. You cannot be much more abstract than to say that national growth is an issue. However, as part of that question, there are a lot of very important friction points that we are going to see coming out in this decade. I think that one of the most obvious ones is going to be the issue of continued economic growth versus the environmental problem. There is already developing a collision course between the people who are advocating continued low unemployment and rapid job development on the one hand and the people who are tending to the other extreme by demanding that industries which appear to be guilty of thermal pollution be closed down and by attempting to impede further urban growth to the greatest extent possible.

I am posing extremes for you, but it is my feeling that these two interests are going to crystallize more in the next decade and will come up against each other with considerable smoke and maybe fire. I think another issue which is a vital one, and on which this Administration has tried to make some tentative headway, is what I would call a remedy for the arthritis of government. Dr. Gilmour both in the classroom and here has noted the problem of the President being checkmated, but it is not just the President himself who is often checkmated under the present system. It is the congressman, the citizens, the mayor, the state governor who is rendered helpless. What we find is such a proliferation of levels of government, and special units of government, that people trying to respond to regular, ordinary, everyday problems have a difficult time doing so. I think that one thing that we are going to see in the next decade, speaking categorically, is that the New Deal is dead. The New Deal being, strictly speaking, a Federal Government response on nearly every level, for almost every problem, is no longer viable. I think we have seen the rise and the fall of the "Great Society."

What we will see emerging over the next decade is the aftermath of the New Deal, a response by our people to the growing recognition that the central government cannot adequately solve every problem of a social, physical nature. I believe we will see a new role emerging for the private sector. I have highlighted here just three or four of the main issues. Let me very quickly go into just a bit more detail.

Let us return to the issue of growth. The experts on population differ on the estimated number of people that we can expect in our country over the next 20 or 30 years. The typical sort of benchmark is an added 75 million by the end of the century. Interestingly, a large proportion of those numbers will continue to be from immigration. Twenty percent of the annual increase to the American population continues to come from immigration. This is a fact that a lot of people do not realize nor do they realize that population growth will be something like 75 million in the next three decades.

On the question of business growth, our national goal research staff has told us that in the next decade alone between the government and the private sector approximately one trillion dollars worth of new plants and equipment is going to be constructed and located. The President summarized the questions on this issue in a message that he sent to Congress two years ago on population growth and the American future. At that time he set up the Rockefeller Commission on population growth, and he directed it to deal with two main questions. One: should growth, in terms of numbers of people, be encouraged, slowed, or maintained at the present level? What should our public policy be in handling millions more people in the country? Two: More importantly, how can we accommodate whatever kind of growth actually does happen? How are our institutions going to adapt to the growth that we can expect?

I have been serving as the staff director for a Cabinet Committee on national growth policy and we have been beginning to explore these questions. We have looked, for instance, at the work that has been done on something like optimum city size.

Is there a best size for a city? Is there a size for a city beyond which you cannot have economies of safety, beyond which ordinary social problems become more and more complicated and costly to solve. We have been getting into questions about whether or not there should be a national population distribution policy. Should we encourage a lot of new communities or a more rapid growth in some parts of the country as opposed to others, in order to reach people who now have a very low level of income? These are the kinds of issues that we are getting into right now and that will be emerging even more clearly in the next five or six years.

The second thing that I mentioned is what I call the arthritis of government or the unresponsiveness of government. There is a man here today from the staff of the Citizens Committee for Government Reorganization, James Finch. The Citizen Committee was the group that the President asked to come in, in Hoover Commission style, to look at how the whole Federal executive role could be reorganized, and reordered more efficiently. That is just one piece—putting our own house in order.

There is going to be a problem in many jurisdictions in the Congress and in the Senate; their house is not in order yet. There is going to be the problem of what we call intergovernmental relations. Right now the Federal Government is about the most complicated thing that you can consider from the point of view of the local government or a state government. As Daniel Patrick Moynihan used to say, if you put yourself in the position of a mayor, and look up at the Federal Government, with all those hundreds of categorical programs, you feel a little bit like you are under water looking up at the surface on which is a Portuguese man-of-war with thousands of tentacles hanging down toward you. Needless to say you are not sure that you really want to grab any one of them.

Finally, let us consider the question of this new role in public policy in the public sector. It started with the contract performance method of providing education. This may turn out to be a very direct assault on the whole system of public schools. We are saying for the first time "Let us use government money in a performance oriented way. Let us contract with private businessmen to provide schooling for youngsters; and let us hold these contractors accountable for how they do with the end product, with the level of attainment of their students." This is a very radical idea and it is being tried only on a very experimental basis, now, but it may be indicative of a whole new trend in partnership between the Federal Government and the private sector.

On this point, too, we are going to see in the next year in this Administration, and certainly in subsequent administrations, a very heavy emphasis on new technology and how it can be made to work for people in their own everyday town, city, and community problems. Things like waste disposal, security, and police protection, and mass transit will all be considered from this prospect. There is a heightened emphasis in the last year within the Administration on this approach and we have brought into the White House a new special consultant on the application of technology to domestic problems, Mr. William Magruder. I think we are going to see a real escalation of interest in this area.

Here, again, what we may be talking about ultimately, is a role for the Government relating to the private sector almost as big and important as the role of defense activities has been since the beginning of the cold war. Our priorities are changing and our whole system of relationships will change with that. That is just highlighting, and I would like very much to come back to these points when we have gone around the panel. I have not gone at all into the machinery of policy-making, one of the points that interests Dr. Gilmour, and I would like to come back to that too.

EDWIN GILMOUR: Thank you, John. I think you have given us an excellent overview of the challenges and issues in policy that face us in this decade. I think you have illustrated well how the staff operates at the White House level.

I would like to come now to the second major level of presidential assistance, which is the Cabinet and independent agency ring. I agree with everything that Dr. Hoxie said about Mr. William J. Casey, one of the founders of this Center, a most able attorney and public servant. I think that he exemplifies the highest traditions of what I would call responsible businessmen who bring to the public sector the skills and talents that they use so successfully in the private sector. Currently Mr. Casey is Chairman of the Securities and Exchange Commission, and I am sure that he will have some unique insights.

WILLIAM J. CASEY: Addressing the subject of the domestic policy of the 1970's, I would like to start out by saying that this country has a lot of things that it has to accomplish in the 1970's. The President has laid out a plan to achieve many of the main objectives. Basic to our national well-being and to world stability is a healthy economy. We have never had a healthy economy without having a vigorous capital market. The economists on the Federal Reserve Board say that by 1980 to achieve our economic goals, to meet public needs, and to achieve the kind of growth that our economy will require, we shall need nearly $15 billion a year in new equity capital. To grasp that figure you need to understand that 1968 was the first year in which we ever raised more than $3 billion in new equity. Today new equity capital is being raised at the rate of $8 billion a year. Therefore, in order to achieve the kind of goals that the President has set for the economy, we are going to have to double the rate at which public savings are mobilized and brought into capital uses to meet economic needs over the decade of the 1970's.

Let us look at the other side of the equation, the international economy. This, too, is important because where we stand and how we perform as a nation in international competition, will have a great deal to do with the kind of living standards and the kind of economic health we enjoy. Over most of the last decade our currency has consistently been valued at less and we have had to pay more; productivity has gone down; we have shared our technology; other countries have overcome the technological advantage that we had for a good long time during the post war period. I believe that we have come to the end of that period.

With the creation and expansion of the European Common Market we are no longer alone in having a great domestic market on which to base our productivity and economic efficiency. Indeed, we are probably now the second greatest market in the world, the European Common Market ranking first. In addition we must remember that other countries have as great an access to raw materials as we do. All of this comes down to the fact that the last decisive economic advantage we will have may be our ability to mobilize capital. This advantage permits us to carry out things on a larger scale, to exploit technology more rapidly on a larger scale, and to maintain an economic status that permits us to compete in the world. All of this is possible because at the present time 30 million Americans own and participate in equity capital by owning stocks and bonds, and about 100 million Americans participate indirectly through pension plans and other investments to have a stake in our securities markets.

To achieve our economic, social, and domestic goals in the 1970's, we are going to have to extend ownership in the American economy to some 50 or 60 million people.

Let me say a few words about the technique by which the investment operation in the American economy is regulated indirectly. As John Price indicated, we have giantism throughout our governmental structure. That giantism is going to have to be broken down; there are going to have to be more partnerships between the public sector and the private sector.

Within the stock exchanges there are the broker-dealers; who have a process of self-regulation, where, in fact, they regulate themselves, subject to oversight and review by a governmental body. It is interesting that we are generally losing faith in the effectiveness of huge government bodies. When we look at responsibility within the private sector, we find this process of self-regulation also under attack.

Difficulties in self-regulation were encountered in the 1969-1970 period; this is something that will be examined by Congress over the balance of this year and next year to determine whether self-regulation can be effective or whether it requires direct government regulation. That would call for a huge expansion and reorganization of governmental staff. These combined staffs would probably have about four times as many people as the present Securities and Exchange Commission. In brief, if we abandon this concept of self-regulation, we would be going in a direction which has already proved inefficient. Other areas of government have already departed from this type of an over-all structure, moving to the decentralization of responsibility.

One further effect on which I might comment is, that, unlike the other instrumentalities of government represented here, in this round table, the Securities and Exchange Commission is an independent commission, an independent administrative agency. Instead of being dependent upon one source of authority and responsibility, (such as the Presidential assistants and Cabinet officers are to the President), it depends upon *two* sources, namely both the President and Congress.

All of these administrative agencies—the FCC, the SEC, and

ICC,—are basically answerable to the Congress. Within all these bodies, there is a multiplicity of functions. But in the case of the Securities and Exchange Commission, there is an administrative function of information about the securities that are sold to the public, a legislative function of framing rules which are administered by the Commission, an investigatory and a prosecution function, and also an additional function of regulating the groups that come under these rules.

I believe that this is typical of the whole important area of administrative regulation which governs the communications industry, the large part of the aviation industry, and the power industry. They are all under this kind of review and regulation. As independent agencies of government they are responsible both to the Congress and to the President.

EDWIN GILMOUR: Thank you, Chairman Casey. You have spoken, most clearly and most effectively to what is obviously a central concern of all Americans. I am also grateful that you pointed out the unique status and functions of the independent regulatory commission, as an important element in the formulation and execution of domestic policy.

Our next panel member represents the most visible of the President's policy assistants, namely, the member of the Cabinet. James M. Beggs, Under Secretary of the Department of Transportation, is a graduate of the U.S. Naval Academy. After seven years of service in the Navy, Mr. Beggs served for 13 years in top management of the Westinghouse Corporation. In June 1968, he entered the government through NASA and moved into his present position in March, 1969.

JAMES M. BEGGS: Thank you, Professor Gilmour. I would like to take off a little bit from where John Price ended, and maybe cover a little ground already covered in his presentation. Then I will talk about some of the problems of transportation as related to concerns he voiced.

Transportation has been largely an unplanned kind of activity, although it has, throughout this nation's history since the origin of the Republic been a rather unique partnership between Federal, State and local government and private industry. Now we come to the latter half of the 20th Century, and find ourselves in a state of transportation crisis, in a state of urban crisis to which the transportation system should be directing itself.

Unfortunately in the past, and indeed in the present time, there is no broad framework of government policy in which one can define a transportation policy or housing policy or any of the other policies which relate to urban development. That is, there is no rational growth policy, there is no general policy planning in this country related to the question of what it is that we are after, what the broad objectives are, what the intent of the federal policy is, and how that meshes with the local and state objectives. As a consequence of that, we have not yet succeeded in relating our domestic departments to the rather broad authority we have to spend money.

The Transportation Department employs 106 thousand people; it spent this year alone, 8½ billion dollars, mostly with state and local jurisdiction. It is the third largest of the executive departments in terms of employment, and I believe it is fourth or fifth largest in terms of the amounts of money that it spends. Yet in spite of that, and in spite of the fact that our investments on the federal level have been very large, it has not succeeded in relating itself to the problems in the urban areas. That is what we are chiefly talking about when we are talking about transportation. That is where 80% of our people live, and that is where the major problems of transportation exist.

There are four major issues related to the basic structure of government and the way that it operates. Let us deal with the structure of the Federal Government, first. The President is constrained and restrained in his dealings with domestic policies. The Federal Government itself is organized and structured in such a way that it cannot really relate to a number of different categories in this area. There are at least five of the Federal executive departments which relate directly to the problems of the urban area, and the coordination of those departments is very difficult.

As you know, the President has made a proposal for reorganization of the Federal Government, which is long overdue. At the very least, the Government should try to organize in such a way that it brings together all of the categories of aid and assistance, and all the categories of policy-making and study, if it is to have any chance to solve the problems.

The second problem is related, which is the problem of the Congress itself. Congressional reorganization is also long overdue. I will not be so bold as to suggest to the Congress that they reorganize themselves. I will suggest that the kinds of problems that most of the executive departments have to deal with in this present Congressional organization prevent effective conjunction of a number of programs addressed to the problems of the urban system. The worst of these examples is the Department of Transportation, itself. This department reports to, gives testimony before, and must, in one way or another, be subject to the jurisdiction of 23 different Congressional committees.

The third problem, is that of local systems. State and local jurisdictions have been unable to structure themselves in such a way that they can effectively attack the problems created by multiple jurisdictions. I am told that if you stand on top of the Empire State Building, you can see some 11 or 12 hundred individual political jurisdictions. The same is true, of course in almost every major metropolitan area in the country. Not only do these community authorities cover multiple jurisdictions within one state but in many cases they cover jurisdiction within two or three states, such as the Port of New York Authority. That presents several problems for the effective development of policy, and for the implementation of the system within that policy and the planning process necessary for the long range cyclical system. The problems of our transportation are in this instance but representatives of this complicity. I submit that we must find a better organizational structure in the local and state jurisdiction.

The fourth difficulty, of course, is the availability of financing, or the availability of investment within this structure. Here again we have categorized and departmentalized our financial help for state and local jurisdictions to the extent that if a state or local jurisdiction wants to put together a total plan to attack its urban problems it is simply unable to cut its way through the multitudes of governmental red tape at the Federal level and, indeed, at the state level as well.

Within the concept of the problems related, let us look specifically at Transportation. There are two or three major transportation issues related to the urban system. One is the question of highways and how far we can go with our highway development in this country. The second is the question of public transportation and how far we can go to subsidize or improve public transportation so that it can provide for most of the individuals who need mobility within the urban area. This requires a balance between the modes. The third problem is the relationship of private transportation and public transportation with the other parts of the urban system; housing, the educational system, the health system, the cultural amenities, etc.

We have a number of different options in this country. The system that we have in place has served the nation well. But it has become outmoded as the complexities of the urban system increased and it has become, in some of the modes of transportation (e.g. public transportation) completely unworkable. However, there is a basis to build, and we had better start moving on this in a more urgent fashion. It would appear from the normal growth that we have in mobility demand in this great country, that we are probably far behind the power curve in adding to capacity. For the last several years, we have been investing about 25 to 30 billion dollars a year in the part of our transportation assets relating to infrastructure. That is three percent of the current Gross National Product, and it is about four percent of the total value, of the total investment capital, that has been put into that transportation system in the last 200 years. That total runs about 500 billion dollars.

The question is, how are we going to attract the capital into an industry which has been under capitalized and currently is in financial difficulties, because it does not earn sufficient financial return? Secondly, how are we going to lay the basis for a viable system within the metropolitan areas that will truly look far enough ahead to enable us to build the infrastructure that will provide the mobility that will be necessary 10 years hence?

The system in the urban area requires a decade or more to plan and bring into operation. Indeed, it has required even longer than that in the past. We are working a ten or twenty year problem with a two or a three, or at most, a four year planning cycle.

Finally, one has to turn to other problems that are related to the *basic operation* of this system. Transportation has been considered a monopoly so that it has, by virtue of legislation and statutes, necessitated the over-regulation of these industries. We now have modes that compete rather vigorously with each other, such as trucks, waterways, railroads, etc., for domestic transport. The air mode and marine mode compete in the coastal and international transportation area. We still treat each one of them as a monopoly needful of the large federal and state regulatory structure and ponderous procedures which inhibit action. I submit that this needs complete rethinking.

The second problem, of course, is the aforementioned question referred to by Mr. Casey of how we are going to attract investment capital into the industry without burdening the industry with even more federal regulations by requiring increased federal expenditures in such areas as intra-city transportation, public transportation, and inter-city transportation in the high-population corridors, as in the Northeast.

Third, we must consider what and how we are going to re-establish a balance of transportation to reduce over-all reliance on private transportation in our cities. There, the problem of congestion in commuter traffic and the problem of pollution resulting as well as an impending energy crisis comprise one of the great problems of our society today. But how does one return a balance to that while at the same time providing the same degree of mobility to the population that they have enjoyed and seem to demand in the present? Currently, about 92% of the passenger trips in the metropolitan areas are made by private auto. Less than eight percent rely on public transportation. Certainly, one has to look out for the next two or three decades to provide a stabilizer for that rather imbalanced situation.

Lastly, is the question of providing for the local and state governments some flexibility and some ability to use the funds that they have available in a flexible way to solve problems as they see them. We started speaking some time ago in the area of transportation about providing a transportation trust fund or a transportation account. The President, as you know, has proposed revenue sharing to the Congress. This proposal would provide flexibility for the state and local jurisdictions and would transfer to them the three modes. This flexibility is absolutely essential for the local jurisdictions and their leadership so that they can observe and solve the problems as they see them according to their individual situation.

The problem of the next two or three decades will be in finding a way to adapt or modify the institutions we have created in the past in such a way as to provide flexibility for local problem solving, because more than ever local definition and solutions will become critical. The Federal Government, I submit, does not have either the foresight or, indeed, the means of solving these institutional changes for the local governments. Thank you.

EDWIN GILMOUR: Thank you, Secretary Beggs. We are indebted to you for describing the whole constellation of transportation problems that increasingly plague our urban, industrial society. Also, you have demonstrated the difficulties and frustrations in trying to adapt a governmental system that evolved in the latter part of the 18th century, when our society was overwhelmingly rural and our economy predominantly agricultural, to the new social and economic realities of the twentieth century.

Another representative of the cabinet departments is Robert A. Podesta, the Assistant Secretary for Economic Development in the Department of Commerce. Mr. Podesta came to the Nixon Administration after a long and very distinguished career in the business world as a nationally-prominent investment banker. His main base of operation was in the Chicago area. Mr. Podesta.

ROBERT A. PODESTA: Thank you, Dr. Gilmour. I think the least understood activity in the Federal Government is the budget process. In my own estimation, half of the Congress does not understand it, and I may be being charitable. For instance, in the Economic Development Administration we have a small Indian program. Among the recent spate of books about the Indians was one entitled *Custer Died for Your Sins* by Vine DeLoria, Jr. In it he says, "It would be fair to say that of any agency in the government in the last few years EDA has been the most responsive to tribal programs." When you realize that EDA spends about $25 million annually on Indian Affairs and the Bureau of Indian Affairs spends $500 million, you must wonder why the Indians feel EDA is most responsive. It is because we are allowed to do things that the BIA cannot do. I grant you it should not be that way, but that is the way it is.

EDA can spend its money on Indian reservations for many things—putting a fence on the Mescalero reservation to better control their cattle herd—building a plant in Shiprock, New Mexico, where Fairchild Hiller conducts a large operation making semi-conductors—or helping the Lummi Indian Tribe get into the aquaculture business. While these are all worthy projects, perhaps the biggest need on the reservations is for planning money. We send over to OMB a request for what in Washington is a tiny additional amount for this purpose—$1.2 million. This added to our present authority would give us enough to make planning grants to all Indian reservations. Whereupon someone asks, "Why don't you take this out of the overall $25 million that you expect to spend anyway?" And the answer is, literally, that we cannot do it because our appropriation is given to us on what is known as a "line item" basis. We cannot transfer from one line item to another.

I am over-simplifying this to say that most of the people out in the business world, or even the academic world, would be more consistent and more helpful if they understood the constraints under which Jim Beggs operates, for example. For instance, he cannot spend any money at the moment as far as we know on Indian reservations for roads. That is what Rogers Morton told the Indians yesterday. That is the way the law reads.

It does not seem to make sense because if there is one thing the Indians need on the reservations it is roads and better transportation, and yet we arrange it so the big Department of Transportation cannot even talk to—and in fact, is not even represented at—the Indian meetings.

I have another thing to say about roads. Some of the people are road happy! For instance, the Appalachian Regional Commission gets more money for Appalachia than EDA does for the entire country. While Appalachia extends into 13 states including New York, it includes only one entire state—West Virginia. But what do they do with their money? In West Virginia they build a lot of highways. What happened in the last 10 years in the census? West Virginia lost more population than any other state in the Union. In other words, the ARC built a lot of roads and everybody left!

The Economic Development Administration has a very broad mandate but not very much money to carry it out. EDA has $250 million budgeted annually to promote "economic development" throughout the entire nation, which in a trillion dollar economy is not very much.

Pat Moynihan initiated the Washington Conference on National Growth, to which I was invited, by saying to all the Ph.D's who were sitting there that he had invited Secretary Podesta because as far as he could tell, they were all on the EDA payroll. He was referring to the grants that we give to universities so that great scholars can study basic questions about regional economic development.

The President has said that one of the big problems for the 1970's—and he said it in his 1970 State of the Union message—is that we have to do something about this imbalance between the cities and the rural areas. Incidentally, there is a new word for cities. They are not megalopolises any more; they are conurbations. I thought it sounded a little indecent the first time I heard it.

But even if we spend all the money provided, can we solve all the problems of the cities? The Federal Government has been pouring funds into the cities, so in creating EDA and its predecessor, the Area Redevelopment Administration, the intent was to do something about the rural areas of the country. But the Congress—once they found that EDA appeared to be working rather effectively—changed the rules so that we now have to direct a part of our efforts to work on city problems.

Congress extended our organization for two years in a rather offhand way just recently. I think you will be interested in this, it being germane to the budget question. After a bill by which Congress attempted to put $2 billion into accelerated public works was vetoed, Congress turned around and passed a bill which in very broad, loosely-worded language said that we must spend at least 25 percent, but not over 35 percent; and incidentally extended EDA for two years and ARC for four years (these two programs being the darlings of the Congress). In effect, this is a program somewhat like the public works projects of the New Deal. Congress wants to find out if we can, in fact, start projects quickly enough to put people to work in specific places, and so do a lot of people. OMB is watching this program very carefully.

Incidentally, the big cities have very able economic development staffs. In my own opinion, Chicago has the number one staff, and New York has second best. Recently, we had to go out and tell Seattle that they were going about their problems in the wrong way. Then we were able to make a grant to Seattle to set up a staff along the lines of Chicago and New York. We are now talking to the Governor of Michigan about a special statewide planning program.

I find that everybody is concerned these days with the "problems of the '70's," and the rules change minute by minute. The new stock answer to all these problems is *revenue sharing*. And you must realize that as a part of the Executive Branch one is not allowed to express his own opinion about matters once the signals have been called from the White House. So when the White House says "We're going for revenue sharing," everybody is for it and believes it will pass. We are all on one ball club, and while it sometimes gets frustrating, there is only one way to play. If you believe the decision is wrong and get caught lobbying against it, you will be back in Chicago or wherever you came from very quickly. On the other hand, if you are really fairly sure that any particular program will not pass, good staff work requires that you begin preparing alternatives.

Over-riding everything else is the fact that '72 is coming up. There are those who say both about any administration and the Congress that in a national election year there is no real concern for the public interest. They say that the second principle of every elected official is, "anything that will serve to get me re-elected is right." That is the second principle, and the first principle is always subject to the second principle. I do not believe that charge can be made against this Administration.

EDWIN GILMOUR: Mr. Secretary, you have remarked both positively and entertainingly, on the restraints placed on presidential policy-making by the executive bureaucracy and also by the Congress. We are grateful to you.

Another member of the departmental sector of presidential assistants is a young man who, happily, can speak from two important but different perspectives. Mr. Ray B. Chambers, Deputy Assistant Secretary for Community and Field Services, Department of Health, Education and Welfare, is a graduate of the University of California at Redlands. Before he was appointed to his present position in August of this year, he served as a staff aide in the U.S. House of Representatives. Hence, he brings to this panel discussion the unique insights of both an executive assistant and a legislative assistant. Mr. Chambers.

RAY B. CHAMBERS: I find myself in an interesting, difficult position sitting at this table with such esteemed personages as the President's personal representative and the Acting Secretary of the Department of Transportation. The Secretary of the Department of Transportation is currently out of the country, which makes Mr. Beggs Acting Secretary.

In a more humble way I know how he feels. My boss is Patricia Reilly Hitt, the Assistant Secretary of H.E.W. for Community and Field Services and one of the top ranking women in Government. When she leaves Washington, I become the Acting Assistant Secretary, which may make me one of the acting top women in government! I will tell you that is when acting is really necessary.

My department—Health, Education and Welfare, is the largest in the Federal Government, with the exception of the Department of Defense. We have over 250 operating programs, and we spend better than $70 billion a year including the budget of the Social Security Administration. We employ directly about a hundred and ten thousand persons, although this is going to be reduced slightly over the next year. It is an enormous, complicated task to manage this holding company of government programs.

I want to speak to you now on what I see as the Department's long-range strategy. My first three points will revolve around health, education, and welfare. My last point will relate to the mechanics of administration in achieving our goals. These Departmental initiatives I will discuss are in direct response to the President's initiatives and the presidential priorities.

The New Deal, to which John Price referred, of course was initiated during the Roosevelt era when government recognized that it had an obligation to do something about the social and economic problems of the time. The New Deal came to full fruition in the Johnson era with a proliferation of categorical programs.

I joined the Congress as a staff member in June of 1963; I left it in April of 1971. When I joined, there were some 40 or 50 categorical grant programs operating in the Federal Government. At the time of my departure, there were nearly 470 categorical programs. There has been a tremendous proliferation of categorical programs within the Government. To grapple with this the Nixon Administration is attempting to, first of all, create mechanisms that will move Government decision-making back to the local level. Secondly, it is trying to harness other resources within private sectors of the economy to make policy and programs work better for people.

I will move now to my first three points—health, education, and welfare. This Administration has taken the position, which undoubtedly will be accepted under future administrations, that all people in this country have a right to a basic level of health care. A health strategy is being developed whereby all citizens will be covered with some kind of insurance; and where better medical care will be available either through health maintenance organizations or other structures. In Education, during the decade of the 70's, I see an equalization of financing for our school systems around the country. Certainly the California court decision, which basically rejects the principle of property tax, may well be an important element in the future of our educational systems. It is my opinion that the contribution of the Federal Government is going to be largely through a general system of educational revenue sharing, moving sharply away from the categorical approach.

In the area of welfare, there is the Welfare reform package. I believe that a package similar to that which was passed by the House of Representatives with broad bi-partisan support will, in fact, become the law of the land, hopefully by the end of this Congress or during the next one. This program will establish a new principle of federalized welfare with some state assistance to bring people up to a higher level of income in the higher income states. Congress may argue about the amounts, but I believe the principle is going to be established as the new wave of the future.

Finally, on the question of governmental management and governmental organization or reorganization, I see our departments being put together in a more logical fashion. This will occur through the Reorganization Act, which I feel is eventually going to pass Congress in some form or another. I also see decision-making being moved from Washington, D.C. to the local communities and mechanisms being created to make that happen. To elaborate on that, let me state the broader perspective first and then elaborate on all of these major initiatives that I have talked about, primarily revenue sharing, welfare reform, health initiatives, and reorganization. These *are* Nixon Administration programs and some of them *are* in trouble with Congress. However, I feel very deeply that just as Franklin Roosevelt began the New Deal, that Richard Nixon is beginning a new trend in government that will not be reversed—regardless of administration.

There is not a presidential candidate on the horizon, of either party, who does not have a revenue sharing program of one kind or another built around the principle of the Nixon Administration program. Most of the presidential candidates are supporting welfare reform proposals along the general lines of the present welfare reform proposal. All the presidential candidates have adopted a proposal for some sort of comprehensive health coverage. They range, of course, from the Kennedy plan of federalization of health delivery to the American Medical Association plan of private incentives. Organized labor also has a plan, and there are a variety of others. Health Reform is going to come.

These basic initiatives, these new thrusts in the areas of Health, Education, and Welfare, are going to become, in my opinion, a fact of life. We have started something new in this Administration that is going to continue.

Finally, the process of administering an organization as enormous as H.E.W. is somewhat overwhelming.

I believe that this Administration in the last two years has taken some administrative initiatives that are very important to making government work. Regionalization is an important aspect of that. This Administration has established for the human resource agencies 10 standard Federal regions out of scores of Federal regions that existed. The Departments of Transportation, HEW, HUD, the Environmental Protection Agency, OEO, and LEAA are locating together in these ten regions. Concurrently with that, each agency—some more than others—has made a major effort to move decision-making authority to the regional directors of those agencies and to give them more flexibility in administering their programs. Also, regional councils have been created in each of these ten areas. These councils are comprised of the regional directors or designated representatives of each of the human resource Departments. They sit down together every week and see how they can work better jointly to deliver programs more effectively within their regions.

There have been a large number of other initiatives in the decentralization area. Of major significance is the trend toward broadening programming responsibility in the field while meshing our priorities with those of local and state governments.

I believe that in the domestic field we have started a new thing in this Administration, and that we are moving in an exciting direction.

EDWIN GILMOUR: Thank you, Ray. You have done an excellent job, not only of commenting on current domestic policies from your own departmental point of view, but you have also emphasized the important reality that the President operates not only as the administrator of existing policy, but also, at the same time, plays the role of policy innovator. Too, you have noted the developing trend within the Nixon Administration toward a more decentralized, more coordinated inter-governmental pattern.

To wrap up the panel presentations, I am going to call upon an academic, a person with both an informed and a detached point of view. This man was a long time Professor of Political Science at Duke University. In 1966, he came to Columbia University, where he has served first as the Director and now as the President of the Academy of Political Science. During this long period of educational service, he has also, periodically and effectively, served in a consultant capacity to the Bureau of the Budget, the Department of the Navy, and, in more recent years, at the metropolitan governmental level. I think he has a splendid perspective for concluding this panel discussion. Let me introduce Dr. Robert H. Connery, Professor of Political Science and President of the Academy of Political Science at Columbia University.

ROBERT H. CONNERY: I wondered why Dr. Hoxie was so careful not to identify me as a college professor. He introduced me as Dr. Connery, the President of the Academy, but it was not until now that I was unmasked as a college professor. The reason became quite obvious this morning when George Reedy was talking. You will recall at one point he said, "Well, on the one side of the table you have the full weight of the government, and on the other, perhaps a college professor." College professors do not carry weight. I can only think of one man who consistently keeps telling me that I am carrying too much weight in the world and that is my doctor. My confidence was further undermined by Mr. Reedy when a little later he was referring to an adversary situation and he said on "the one hand you have the Government and on the other hand you have a nitpicker." Seeing that he went too far, he hastened to amend that he did not dislike college professors. I am quoting Mr. Reedy correctly, simply out of context, perhaps exercising not the freedom of the press, but the freedom of the platform. On occasion, I do not have too much sympathy for freedom of the press. Mr. Hagerty, however, gave me a role. He said that even in higher circles of the Government, the professor is apt to be in effect a sort of devil's advocate, the man who, whether he believes in them or not, would raise objections and see that they were discussed.

So after being deflated by Mr. Reedy, Mr. Hagerty gave me a better role and what I intend to do in the three or four minutes that remain is to raise some questions that I think we ought to be considering. These are the questions that a political scientist, indeed a professor of political science, might ask a panel of distinguished government officials who do carry a considerable weight in the world. We seem to be in agreement that domestic problems, and in the area of domestic problems, urban problems, are the major ones for the 70's; problems of mass transportation, education, health, housing, and control of capital. I am glad that my colleagues did not describe in great detail what these programs would be in this decade. I think we are familiar enough with these topics that we need not spend too great a deal of time discussing them.

But there are some other questions. It is obvious that the Federal Government already is spending a great deal of money for education, health and highways. I wonder what we are getting for our money. Are we, in the words of President Johnson, becoming a more healthy nation? My colleagues here can speak to that point.

With all these millions of dollars and these 106,000 employees in the Department of Transportation, are we getting any better transportation system? How can the results be evaluated? Who is evaluating them? What is the role of the President in these new programs, which are largely unplanned, I assume, from the comments so far? Do these programs come primarily from the bureaucracy? Is it true that the President has taken a public position on such things as grants to the state? Do members of the Administration follow his leadership or do they push ahead of him? Is his role an originator of programs? What is the role of his staff?

To what extent is there a systematic examination of the problems of the country? Is it done in preparation of the State of the Union message? Is it done in preparation of the budget? How do these new domestic programs originate? From whom? From Congress? From the professional bureaucracy? From the White House? What is the White House role, and what is the role of the staff? I do wish that my colleagues would enlighten us a little more on these matters. If the need for these programs on the Indian reservations, in Appalachia, and in the field of health and education are so obvious today, why were they not undertaken previously? Is it a failure in the people who held office, or is it a structural failure? If it is structural, then we ought to know it. If it is individuals, then perhaps our political system of nomination and selection of high officers should be re-examined.

My central question is to what extent are we able to evaluate our present government's activities? Who is to make the evaluations? What is the input and what is the process of the input? Is it structure or individuals? If Mr. Reedy had not needled me this morning, I would not have had any of these great thoughts that I am sharing with you today. I am, in effect, being a devil's advocate, twitting my colleagues a little bit. I hope they can shed some light on these things.

EDWIN GILMOUR: Thank you, Mr. Connery. I, too, winced a bit when Mr. Reedy made those remarks about the groves of academe. But his remark about the weight we professors carry was vague enough that I assumed he meant our midsections were leaner than those of governmental and political colleagues. In any case, as a professor, you have done an excellent job of putting the observations of the panel members into both a broader and sharper focus, through the very pointed questions you have raised.

I am going to ask John Price to respond to some or all of these questions, since as White House Special Assistant, he operates at the most general level. And he has as broad a perspective as anyone on the panel, perhaps with the exception of Dr. Connery himself.

JOHN PRICE: Thank you, Dr. Gilmour. One of the first points

that I would like to make is in reference to all the talk you have heard about the categorical grants and the massive growth of the Federal Government, and then I will go into the process of decision-making. I have what I call "Price's Barnacle Theory of the Federal Government" which is that over the years Federal programs build on each other just as barnacles do to the hull of a ship. I do not know how many of you have scraped barnacles, but it turns out to be literally impossible to do at the Federal Government level. We have an encrusted layer of programs which come to the point where they require coordination beyond your wildest dreams.

Let me just take a few minutes to outline for you a fairly typical Presidential decision-making activity. Let us take, for instance, the health care package which was put together this last winter by Kenneth Reese Cole, Jr. and myself, serving as the White House coordinators. Ken and I created a cabinet level committee on health care which consisted of several of the departmental secretaries and the representatives from the bureau. We then set out with the general problem in mind that we needed both to meet the payment needs of people for their health care, and to improve greatly the pattern of delivery of health services within reasonable cost. Ken more or less supervised the insurance side, and I supervised the delivery side. We held a couple of initial meetings on the cabinet level, including one with the President, to get a general impression of the kinds of things the President would be willing to go along with and the kinds of things he was reluctant to support. In that way, we got a further concept of Mr. Nixon's attitude toward a health program.

From there each of the Cabinet members designated one or more from their departments to meet initially on a weekly basis and later on a daily basis, increasing to hours and hours each day, with Cole and myself. The initial responsibility for stating the problem, for putting a price tag on solutions to it and so forth, lay with the various departments. Our role was really as ringmasters in that process. They would come into us with drafts, and we would then say that this looks good or that does not, or is not that costing too much? We would then, after refining the draft, take it back to the Cabinet group and have them go through it, giving them their own recommendations and their strong feelings, if there were any. Finally a decision paper was drafted for the President which reflected a very careful analysis of the majority of recommendation and any dissenting views.

You have heard a lot of arguments from George Reedy for one example, that any President is isolated. This is very true. In some respects, it is even more true of a personality as reserved as Richard Nixon. He is a very personal man. He does not go out and meet and greet people the way other Presidents have habitually done. However, he does insist before any major decision is made, such as the health program or the welfare program, upon having it very clearly stated in the decision paper where his people stand. I mean by his people not just his White House staff whispering in his ear, but initially his departmental people. In the welfare decision, as in the health decision, the President put together not just a decision paper, but a lot of back-up materials for reading. He consulted a lot of outside people—personal friends, experts whom he knew or whom his staff suggested to him—purposely trying to get into that group as broad a spectrum of people as he could. The reactions of these people were included as well in the final package that would go into the decision paper.

The President then, in the case of Richard Nixon, is apt to retire behind closed doors and to read these documents, and then he may return to us asking for an oral argument on the brief. In that case, we would pull together a Cabinet level meeting with him. He would then sit down and go over the decision paper with the cabinet members and have them stress in more detail their reluctance to go along with certain points or their strong positive recommendations.

That is fairly characteristic of the process in which major decisions are made. The other ones are short of that, and in those he relies very heavily upon his internal staff or upon the individual cabinet officer who has the main interest in it.

Let me stress that this process is a little different from what has gone on before. The President has adopted the pattern of the National Security Council for domestic policy formation, and so he has created this formal body called the Domestic Council. The papers that I mentioned to you are most often developed by what we call sub-groups of the Domestic Council. The Domestic Council has a staff in the White House. It is larger than the past domestic staffs of any president. We now have probably 16 to 18 professionals in the White House who directly assist the President in these kinds of decisions. We find, despite the apparent arguments to the contrary, that Cabinet members since the institution of the Domestic Council are really very deeply involved in the decisions, even those that do not directly concern their own departments.

Let me give you an example of that. I served as the staff director of the Cabinet Committee on the Model Cities Program. We learned a great deal from taking five Cabinet members through a whole model cities process. I say this advisedly because the model cities project is as much a process as it is a program. After we had had three or four half-day sessions at Blair House, George Romney, who was the Chairman of that committee, came to me and said, in essence: "Model cities is run by my Department, but here you have the Secretary of Transportation, you have the Secretary of Labor, you have the Director of the Poverty Program, and you have the Secretary of HEW at these meetings. I've been interdepartmentalized to death!" This is, perhaps, the critical side of it, but the positive side of it is that someone like the Secretary of Transportation, who has intimate interest in the inner city and its problems through mass transit questions and through the questions of the balance between highway funds and public transportation funds is involved in those decisions. This is new.

Perhaps the Johnson Administration did this as a matter of course, but this President insists on it. Unless he is assured that the process has been followed, he will simply say: "I'm sorry, I need to have the views of x and y before I make my decision on this." That, in summary, is how it works. The Office of Management and Budget, about which you will hear more tomorrow, is an "honest broker" in these proceedings and is the enforcer, or torpedoer, once those decisions have been made. It will whisper in our ears when it thinks that the departmental cost estimates are absolutely fatuous or when it feels that the program is not being properly represented. It is the enforcer, once the President makes up his mind, in that it is the Office of Management and Budget which on a quarterly basis, will say to those Departments, "I'm sorry, but you are not following the President's program."

Let me give you one caveat on this whole process and one caveat about Presidential power in particular. We have heard about the unbridled power of the President in the foreign policy area. Well, there are very subtle constraints there. We have heard about the much more limited power of the President in the domestic area and the checks and frustrations in that area. Let me tell you just how frustrating it actually can be. Early in this Administration, the President flew over the "temporary" Navy buildings on the Mall in Washington which had been there since 1917 and said, "My God, they were here when I was here at the beginning of World War II; they were here when I was here in the Eisenhower days; and they are still here!" He gave an order to tear them down, and it took only 12 months to get that done. Richard Nixon probably thinks that is the most visible accomplishment of his Administration. That is Presidential power; naked, unbridled, raw Presidential power! Thank you.

EDWIN GILMOUR: John, before I turn to the other members of the panel with some written questions that have been submitted, might I query you briefly about your reference to the Office of Management and Budget? Today, we have identified different layers or rings of presidential assistants, those in the inner core of the Executive Office, those at the departmental or agency level, and then, those on the outside who come in on a temporary basis. What about another dimension? Is there a distinction to be made concerning the personnel within the Executive Office of the President? I would hope you might agree that there are two distinguished groups of personal assistants to the President in the Executive Office. One group consists of people such as the Budget staff and other specialists who are career civil servants. The other group includes people, like yourself, political appointees, who serve as special assistants in the White House Office. I would think that these two different groups come from very different backgrounds and have different orientations and expectations.

JOHN PRICE: Well, as I said a moment ago, OMB, in my view, really is genuinely honest. I think the standard of qualification and ability of the career people in that office, which is a small office of about 400 people in all, is probably as high, on the whole, as any group of people who you would find in any function in the country. Exemplary of them is Dwight Ink, who is with us here this weekend. Dwight was the recipient in 1966 of the Career Service award of the National Civil Service League. Now, however, he serves at the pleasure of the President since he has risen to Presidential appointment rank.

These career service people display a markedly extraordinary sense of loyalty to the institution of the Presidency and to the fact that the President is the one who has to take the heat for all decisions. Their job is to help him in making those decisions. As far as I can see, there is relatively little bias displayed by these people. They are really exemplary in many ways.

The Departments tend to think that beyond being exemplary, the OMB people are often a little over-zealous. However, from the President's point of view, these are his intelligent, strong-arm men. I was asked a question speaking to a group of students yesterday afternoon, about the President's relationship to the various Departments. Here the question that you raised is a little bit more of a problem for the President. In one sense the Departments have the final say on the implementation of a Presidential decision. However, a career man out in Tennessee, who is running a Small Business Administration Office out there, can decide whether he is going to follow the President's policy or whether he is not. By and large, the standard of performance is terrifically high, but these people are more removed from the President. The President cannot see them all the time; they do not understand the shadings of his feelings; and they perhaps do not even understand the main thrust of his program. To some extent, a President can be thwarted in the field by these people.

Now, Washington is a pattern of independent powers. The career people see Presidents come and go; they see Cabinet members come and go; they even see comedians and administrators like Bob Podesta come and go. The fact is that Congress has independent relations to the Departments. The Budget Bureau says: "I'm sorry, you are not going to get that 300 million dollars more for your program." so the career man who happens to know the third ranking Democrat on the Ways and Means Committee will just call up his buddy on The Hill and say: "I have to have the money", and the Congressman will say, "That is what I was going to tell you anyway, so we are going to authorize that now." It is not an easy matter.

The OMB, just to summarize, really is a very important arm for the President.

ROBERT PODESTA: Sometimes we do not think the Office of Management and Budget reads the President's messages. Dr. Connery asked how the State of the Union message gets put together. Right about this time of year we get a request from the Secretary asking if we have any ideas for inclusion in the State of the Union message, and each of the agencies comes up with its ideas for inclusion. Our Department has sent over lots of ideas, but if we get one line in the President's message, we are lucky. And so a lot of things that are in Presidential messages are not originated by the President. On the other hand, for the rest of the year when dealing with OMB we are able to kick off our argument by saying, "As the President said in his State of the Union message," etc., etc.,

Indians are a case in point. I told you EDA could not get a measly million dollars for Indian planning. But we are not alone. Yesterday, the Vice President gathered John Mitchell, Rogers Morton, men from all the agencies, the head of General Motors, and quite a few others in a meeting called to emphasize how much the Administration wants to help the Indians. But I still cannot get a million and a quarter dollars, even with the Vice President pushing it.

I do not know much about the power struggle that has been alluded to or guessed at. It may exist, but the emphasis on it is overblown. All the people around the President are overworked. Every morning at 7:30 these OMB people and these White House guys start the day with a very serious meeting, and they work on into the evening. They are under pressure from all sides, and I sympathize with them, but I still do not think they always read what the President says.

JOHN PRICE: Bob Podesta has faithfully described the making of the Presidential message. The President will finally read it over before it goes to Congress, and, as with the health program, he will have been very much involved in the highlighting of the policy. Nonetheless, he will simply not have the time to focus on some of the specifics. If something is flaring up, such as an Okinawa treaty or Middle East possibilities for peace or even something in the urban area, he may not have the time to focus on every detail. So it is men like myself who fight to be the last one near the mimeograph machine when the stencil is cut the night before the message goes to Congress. I assure you that it is true. I have turned around certain things at 11 PM on the night before the message goes to Congress, and many others have been in a similar position. This is a fact of life.

EDWIN GILMOUR: I have a question here from a newspaper editor, E. S. Harris, directed to Secretary Beggs. The question is: Why not ease the Government restrictions on the ownership of various modes of transportation and let the private sector develop, if possible, coalitions of highway, rail, air and water transportation under one company?

JAMES BEGGS: There is nothing in the statutory regulations to prevent an airline from buying a trucking company or a waterway operator or anything else in the industry. What is in the statutory, regulatory power is the restriction of a railroad from buying any other transportation company. The various commissions, as Mr. Casey explained earlier, have a combined responsibility to the Presidency and to the Congress and in the operations of those statutes. They have effectively prevented the purchase or the establishment of cross-modal transportation companies. We think that in many respects this is bad. However, the issue is not clear; if these restrictions did not obtain, would there, indeed, be better and more fiscally sound transportation? We can only speculate.

In the same form of transportation, such as rail or air, we have had contrary results following mergers, such as Penn Central and Burlington Northern, one very bad, the other very good. But we have no experience for rail systems, for example, running airlines, which they are presently precluded from doing, or of an airline running ships, which they are not presently precluded from doing.

One of the problems in Federal regulation or Federal Program, is that we can most often predict the primary effect of what we do, but we can very seldom predict secondary and tertiary effects. Those are sometimes more important than the primary effects.

One example is the Interstate Highway Program. The program was intended to be economic in direction, with some 42,500 miles of limited access highway construction. As my friend, Pat Moynihan, likes to point out, we ended up with probably the greatest social program this country has ever attempted.

If we intend to change regulations, it should be comprehensive. Indeed we will probably be sending a bill to Congress this session to make significant changes in the regulatory structure. We think the first thing to do in this regard is to make these companies a little more subject to market discipline instead of to the regulatory rate-making of the Interstate Commerce Commission, the Civil Aeronautics Board, and the Federal Maritime Commission.

The objective here is to provide, as in most other countries, e.g. Canada and Australia, a zone of reasonableness in which the companies can react to the market and set rates that are compensatory and offer an adequate return; then maybe you can start talking about some intermodality because nothing prevents anyone, except the railroads, from buying into the other mode. And perhaps we should lift that restriction on the railroad as well. But I think we must first find out if the railroads can be returned to financial health. I submit they are not there now; in the case of the railroads, we must solve the immediate problems before we enter into this question of intermodality.

EDWIN GILMOUR: Thank you, Mr. Beggs. Dr. Daniel E. Brennan of Hunter College makes this statement and asks Chairman Casey to respond. The statement is: "Only profits should be controlled, allowing prices and wages to seek their own level. Would this, perchance, force labor and the consumer to begin to deal, negotiate and function in the world of reality?"

WILLIAM CASEY: I do not think that would work because that would mean that the Government which directs economic activity would dictate where you put your capital, what areas of the economy should expand, and what should contract. You cannot control that segment of the income structure, the profit structure, and let prices and wages float uncontrolled. It has never been tried in the economic history, as far as I know, and I certainly would not want to administer it.

EDWIN GILMOUR: I would like to turn back to Dr. Connery with what I think is really his central question. As I see it, in all the comments and discussions that we have had, not only here, but earlier in this conference, there is clear evidence of general, systemic failure, and the hard question in terms of analysis is, "Where is the failure? Is it personal failure? Is it a structural failure? Or is it a political failure?" And I would like Dr. Connery, as a political scientist with an objective view from the outside, to respond to his own question.

ROBERT CONNERY: Mr. Chairman, I think it is the effect of original sin. In that, I am serious. I am not sure that I agree with the assumption that there has been a failure of the system. We are not going to find perfection. Man is not perfect. Anything he creates is not perfect, and there is not much point in talking about success or failure of government unless you say compared to something. What is the alternative that you have? It is possible, of course, and I was hoping we could move in this direction to evaluate what we are doing and perhaps learn from the past how to improve what we do in the future. I do not know that it is possible to evaluate in the answer to the question I raised here.

We are beginning to plan for the future. But planning has to be based on some evaluation of the past. Government is huge, slow, ponderous and powerful, and there may be comparisons. We have to think what are the alternative successes of other systems. As Mr. Hayden said this morning—in terms of the amount of information available to the American people, and I would add to that, the amount of freedom as government goals, I would evaluate our whole structure of government as far in advance of most, if not all, governments in the world.

If I may just add one phrase, the thing that worries me somewhat, however, is the concentration of power and administration in government at the higher level of government. We keep moving up in the government as a whole, and also in the Federal Government. It seems to me that if Communism fails, as it in my mind has, it is because of an overloading in the system, putting too much control into the government and too many decisions to be made by it.

That is why I was so impressed by Mr. Casey's comment on control of the stock market. I like his concept, and Mr. Nixon's concept, to evolve power and evolve control at the lowest possible level in order to free government, and particularly the Federal Government, to deal with the more important aspects of life. We can improve segments constantly, as we are doing. Then, looking at the system as a whole, I agree that you get failures throughout the system, but on the other hand, you get successes throughout the system, too.

EDWIN GILMOUR: This question is for Mr. Chambers: "Do

the programs now being advocated by your Department represent a real shift from the Government centralization of the New Deal or merely a more efficient administration of such programs?"

RAY CHAMBERS: That is a relatively difficult question for me to answer since I am so close to it. In our office, we are working every day to get more decision-making authority out of Washington and to the regional directors. As a part of that, we are also working to loosen the bindings to decentralize the more than 250 programs we have in the Department of Health, Education and Welfare. However, it is a relatively difficult thing to judge how effective we are.

I am reminded a little bit of a statement that was made by a former Congressman that I am acquainted with. He served several years on the Hill and was appointed by President Nixon to run a large multi-billion dollar bureaucracy. He said he felt an enormous sense of power after having left his modest role as a Congressman with a small staff of eight people and one vote out of 435. There he sat in his big, plushy new office with all the levers and wheels and the brakes of government at his command. He delighted in pushing the levers back and forth turning the wheels and stepping on the brakes. Then, after about three months, he came to the sad realization that all those levers, the wheels and the brakes were not connected to anything! Thus, while I will admit there may be some wheel spinning in the first years of this Administration, I do believe we are moving decision-making slowly, but surely, if haltingly, out to the local units of government.

There remain, however, critical questions, such as that posed by Dr. Connery: i.e. We are spending lots of money on health; we are spending lots of money on education, and all these things, but are we better educated and are we healthier? The answer is probably, yes, we are healthier as a nation, and, yes, we are better educated as a nation.

But who is healthier and better educated as a result of all these expenditures? I am probably healthier and so are you and your family. My wife had a child last May. It was a difficult birth; as a matter of fact, it was such a stormy passage that I would have named her Christopher Columbus Chambers if she had been a boy, but it turned out to be a girl so we named her Elizabeth. During that, my wife and Elizabeth had the very best care available. The oxygen was there; the big complex machinery was there; and the anesthesiologist was standing by. They had that excellent care that minimized the chance of anything going askew—and this, in part, because of research and grants and subsidies made available to the health establishment from the Department of Health, Education and Welfare.

By contrast, last week I was in a barrio in the San Joachin Valley of California, and I visited a man who is trying to begin a health delivery system. There are 5,000 people living in a geographically small community that have practically no health care. The only thing they have access to is a drug store and a county hospital. They have to take a day out of work to get to the county hospital, and then they have to wait in long lines; and because the doctor is overworked the care may not be the best.

Clearly there are inequities in the system, and we must address ourselves to them now. In short, yes we are healthier, but there are people who are still left out. Thus my question is not so much, "Are we healthier" as it is "How do we make it possible for all Americans to buy in?"

ROBERT PODESTA: Once the decision was made to have big government, to decide that government could do something about these various programs, government's role became preeminent. We are never going back, not unless it all breaks down and we find another planet or have another American Revolution. So we ought to quit talking about the welfare state; it is here; and we have got it. What we are trying to do here is manage it better. And that is very unromantic, from a political standpoint.

Let me say a word about the PARC (Planning Assistance Requirements Coordinating Committee). This Committee identified some 36 different planning grant programs, each of which had its own separate sets of forms. So we set to work trying to simplify these procedures. And Chairman Casey is doing the same thing at the SEC. Incidentally, his staff the last time I looked totaled only 1,250 people—which is a darn small staff to handle the securities business nationwide.

Right now personnel shortages are hitting all of us in the Federal Government. The President has instructed us to cut employment by five percent by June 30. One way to do this is through a process known as RIF—for reduction in force. And we also are supposed to accomplish a RIG—reduction in average grade level. Is not government language really something? It is very difficult to handle a RIF and a RIG at the same time, because when you RIF you lose your lower grade people which automatically brings about an increase in the average grade level. It is a nice trick if you can do it, but we are all trying.

JAMES BEGGS: Dr. Connery and John Price raised the question regarding performance and evaluation techniques and where we are going. The truth of the matter is we have no way on the Federal level of determining whether we are performing well, badly or indifferently. We need to have, in most of the new programs we are starting, a method of evaluating as we go along to uncover the secondary and tertiary effects. We need to measure our objectives, and in back of that we need to more fully define our national goals.

DAVID HAIGHT: As a political scientist, I would like to ask a follow-up question to the moderator's question to Mr. Price about the relationship between the career people and the Office of Management and Budget and the procedure of a special assistant brought in by any President. Mr. Price said that he found the OMB staff very professional. I would like to ask Mr. Price what he means by "professionalism" and what effect, if any, professionalism has on relations inside the Government.

JOHN PRICE: By professionalism in this context, David, I meant not only that they were serving the President, but that they were careful, that they were complete, in the range of information they provide, which either supported or counseled against the direction the President looked like he was going to take. By professionalism I refer to the fact that they were, in light of experience, accurate in their analysis of a problem. You will find that they have their own point of view, their *own* institutional view, in what is still based in the Budget Bureau, even though it is called the Office of Management and Budget. They have no hesitation to come out strongly for the elimination of programs which they consider after evaluation to be no longer necessary or productive. And I guess that is what I mean by professionalism in the Office of Management and Budget.

A Cabinet member or a Sub-Cabinet member who comes in at

the President's request very soon finds himself ground between two rocks. One is his desire to serve the President and the other is the fact that he is the guy on the back of the tiger of the department he is trying to run. A department does have its own point of view, its own experts. And a Cabinet member will come pretty quickly to rely upon his people for advice and for information. So he is sort of between the President and his own department. I am not sure it answers your question, except to say I do not mean to slur civil servants in the least, but they do have their own departmental point of view.

JAMES BEGGS: If I can just comment on this briefly, one of the aspects of this, of course, is being responsible. One has to continually remind himself, the commissions and departments, that his responsibility *first* is to the public interest, to the broad public interest, and only secondly to the constituency. And this is hard sometimes, and I think it is particularly hard for the long-term civil servants who are immersed in the problems of their constituency day after day, year after year, 20 or 30 years. It requires a high degree of that kind of professionalism so that the proposals that do float up to the President, that get put before him both by the departments and by the OMB, are objectively presented. John [Price] touched on the fact that this President likes to see *all* of the options. And I think that is very important. I think it is very important that the departments and the OMB have a sufficient level of professionalism where they do not become advocates, but rather present a balanced view and try to surface all of the issues that are related to some new program or some new initiative, so that the President can make a decision that is balanced.

Another thing to be remembered is the fact that the departments are also administering law written by the Congress. I was brought up to think that this is a nation of laws in which the Congress passes the laws which the President executes or implements and that is the law of the land. Many times you get signals from the Executive Branch, even though you are part of it, that are contrary to the law. So you sort of get to feel that the OMB might not be serving the same President you are serving! Your rationale is that you are serving the public! And the poor old OMB hears that from everybody in the Government!

EDWIN GILMOUR: John Price has referred to some real restraints on presidential power. I would suggest that there is another constraint that we have not noted, and I would like someone to speak to the continuing problem of insuring the accountability of public decision-making. Some students of the Presidency have used the term "policy cluster," to refer to a policy conglomerate, centered in the executive civil service but not accountable to the President.

Permit me to give a quick example in the area of farm policy. The leadership of the American Farm Bureau Federation is recognized as one of the most professional and effective of all political interest groups. These men, on a long-term basis, have continuing relationships with the Agricultural Committees in both Houses, more particularly with the permanent staff members of the Committees. The third element in the particular policy conglomerate is the career level of the Department of Agriculture, whose personnel have long-standing working relations with the Farm Bureau staff and the staffers of the Agriculture Committee of the Congress. The basic loyalty of these USDA careerists is to the Congress rather than to the President and to the agricultural interest group rather than to the public. For the Agriculture Committees and the Agriculture Sub-Committees decide the fate of the programs which the USDA administers. And the continuing support of the Farm Bureau and other agricultural interest groups is more important to the USDA than is the support of the general public.

Put all these elements together and you have a "policy cluster," as it has been called, that is not only beyond the control of the President; it is beyond the control of the Congress and, I think it is obvious, beyond the control of the public. Here, then, is a serious and continuing constraint on the President, in terms of power that is irresponsible.

JOHN PRICE: As I indicated earlier, you will find on-going relationships between departmental people and members of their committee on the Hill. And this is real power. The word irresponsible is a very interesting use, because in terms of any national accountability, I guess you are absolutely right. The individual members of the Congress who are on those committees are, of course, responsible to their own constituents and probably speaking for those constituents.

EDWIN GILMOUR: Yes, but they come from safe districts!

JOHN PRICE: Well, I must admit that Jamie Lloyd Whitten from Mississippi on the House Agricultural Committee runs the Agriculture Department for all intents and purposes. I do not know how you wrench away from that. He has served in the Congress since the days of the New Deal. The Congress has been unwilling itself to undertake reforms which would affect those relationships, in terms of changing committee jurisdictions, in terms of changing seniority rules, and so on. That would be one area of reform.

The President has tried to re-jigger the domestic departments to make them more functional and that would, ultimately, I think be a very positive gain for us. People just have to become aware of these special interests. And if they cannot bump off a Congressman that represents one of these interests, then they should try and outnumber him with other Congressmen. You find this happening over a very gradual period of time.

Let us take the agricultural area. The farm price supports is a program of long life now. We find that the public at large is beginning to say now, why should we pay $1.1 million to Senator James O. Eastland of Mississippi for keeping his land out of production or for growing cotton. And so finally what you have for the first time, commencing a year and a half ago in Congress, is a limitation on the payments to individual farmers for either land retirements or for crop allotments. And here you find, gradually, a public awakening to the existence of the very special interests and doing something about it. But it is not something you can change overnight; it takes good journalism, and it takes good political leadership by people who are not captives of that interest.

JAMES BEGGS: It is certainly true that there are clusters of policy-making and programs of special interest in the Government. It is asserted with some justice that the highway program is considered a cluster; there are many others in the Agriculture Department and even in HEW.

There is a corrective mechanism in the system, however, although generally in the past it has taken a long time to operate. The corrective mechanism of booting these guys out does not seem to work. They are there seemingly forever. But the corrective mechanism is, of course, an active and vocal public, and there seems to be growing in this country the various pressure groups in the public sphere, everyone from Ralph Nader to the Indians, if you will, who are surfacing and are pushing very hard points of view which differ from that which had been seemingly held *ad infinitum* in Washington. I think these reformists are working quite well; in fact some of us in Government may think too well! They seem to be working quite well in surfacing these issues and in bringing some pressure to bear in making changes in programs which have gained a powerful constituency and have seemed to go on forever.

If I may, it is about time to tell the story that is making the rounds of Washington which reflects maybe on the bureaucracy in this regard. And since George Reedy apparently is a little hard on academia, this may be a balance. It seems there was a king who lived a thousand years ago, and he was fond of two things. He liked to go hunting and he liked to visit his girl friend. And being as he did not like to get wet, he employed a weather prophet to tell him when the sun was going to shine, so he could go hunting and visit his girl friend. One day, he called the weather prophet, to whom he paid a high salary and who had a suitable retinue, and he said, "What's the weather going to be like?" And the weather prophet looked out the window and there were no clouds in the sky and he peered into his crystal ball and said, "Well, king, the weather is going to be good; you can go hunting and visit your girl friend."

So the king dressed himself in all his finery, got on his white horse, and rode out to go hunting and visit his girl friend. And while he was going down the road, he ran into a farmer who was riding a big flop-eared mule. And the farmer stopped him and said, "King, where are you going?" And the king said, "Well. I'm going hunting and I'm going to visit my girl friend." The farmer said, "You are going to get wet." The king said, "How would you know? He said, "I'm telling you, you are going to get wet and you are going to get very wet." The kind said, "You are crazy; I have a high-priced weather prophet and he said it is not going to rain today, and I'm going on my way."

So he went on, and sure enough it rained and rained very hard; he got very wet, and his clothes shrank and his girl friend laughed at him. He went back to the palace and chopped off the weather prophet's head. He called his prime minister in and said, "Bring me the farmer." So they brought him the farmer and he explained his problem and he said to the farmer, "How would you like to be my weather prophet?" He said, "Well, I'd enjoy that very much, but to tell you the truth, I can't predict the weather." "Of course you can! You told me it was going to rain and it rained." He said, "Well, it was the mule. The mule knows when it is going to rain. You consult his ears. When they lay back against his head, it's going to rain. And when they lay back very hard against his head, it is going to rain very hard." So the king said, "Bring me the mule." So they brought the mule into the palace. So that's how all these high-priced jackasses got into government in the first place.

MARY S. CALDERONE: I am now, too, aware that the private sector can be ahead and well ahead of government in so-called controversial areas. When I went to the Children's Bureau in 1964 to try to get support for the organization which I am now heading, the Sex and Information Council, they looked at me as if to say, "Oh Lord, Mary, you came to us in 1953 for some money for Planned Parenthood, and we've just caught up with that! Now you are 10 years ahead again, and what are you going to do with it?"

In retrospect the lag that the Government displayed in recognition of family planning as a problem of medicine appears sad and ridiculous. And I think this is one of the great signs of President Eisenhower's greatness, that he was able to embrace himself in his first statement in which he said, if you will remember, that birth control is not the business of government but within a year had reversed himself and had become co-chairman of Family Planning along with ex-President Truman.

Now, there is an all too clear parallel to the out-of-hand rejection before careful study or of pigeon-holing of certain reports of governmental commissions because their subjects are controversial or their findings did not fit certain preconceptions. I am referring, of course, to the reports of the task force on homosexuality by the National Institute of Mental Health, a report which is in a pigeon hole, and to the Commission on Obscenity and Pornography. The scientific world is severely shaken by such tactics.

RAY CHAMBERS: I would like to say there is a mark of the success of your program; I only have one child and I only plan one more—at the very most!"

MARY CALDERONE: I am not talking about planned parenthood at all. That problem was won long ago; government is in it. I am seriously asking you a question about prejudgment of findings of serious, highly respected scientists and lawyers and religious people, findings of an official commission that we rejected out of hand purely on the advice of advisors without knowledgeability in the field.

JAMES BEGGS: May I try just a part of this. One of the reasons that the hard scientists have been successful, as you implied, was the fact that several men after the war, headed by Dr. Vannevar Bush and others, went down to Washington and set up a structure that provided for a body of sound advice for the Presidency on scientific issues. And this worked, I submit, very well; in fact, again, some say too well. It resulted in very large scientific programs, some of which are now being challenged as too large expenditures. There is no similar mechanism for the social scientists to advise the President. The National Academy of Sciences of recent years has been trying to attract more of the social sciences into the Academy, to give advice to the President and to render advice to Congress. The Congress, itself, as you know, is very poorly staffed to do this kind of thing for themselves, so they have in the past relied on outside experts and, generally speaking, they trust hard sciences more than they do the soft sciences.

I would suggest perhaps what we have to do in public policy areas is to think harder about mechanisms which would permit the use of nationally-known experts in the various fields of soft sciences in such a way that their findings can be translated into programs. That is the real problem, because the social scientists have found it very difficult. My friend, Guy Stever, President of Carnegie-Mellon, describes that as the task of the social engineer. One of the advantages the hard scientist has is that he has the engineer to translate his discoveries into hardware or systems. We do not have a counterpart of that in the soft sciences. Maybe we need one; but at any event, we do need a structure of government that makes available to the Presidency and to the Congress equally the new findings in the social sciences.

MARY CALDERONE: But meanwhile, if I may comment, I think the Presidency—and I am not speaking of the present Presidency—should be safe-guarded from the kinds of delaying tactics errors that characterized the whole question of family planning and its role in medicine.

JOHN PRICE: Could I please respond on two levels to your question. First of all, this Administration is, I think, the first one to have tried any strategic way to coordinate the soft, or social science research efforts with supporting Federal Government funds throughout its many departments. Dr. Moynihan set up two years ago an inter-departmental committee to do two things: (1) to evaluate research that was being done and had been done; (2) to try and set up a strategy for all departments to follow in the expenditure of their research funds. So we were saying to the departments: do not go idly into areas; here are the kinds of critical areas which are going to be coming up for decision in the next year to four years or five years. So spend your $200 million or more a year, which we do spend in social scientific research, in these kinds of areas, so we will make decisions in an informed way. That is one response.

The second response will sound more cynical; I hope it is not. And that is that politicians are politicians. And you will find that until there is wide acceptability for an idea, the politician is rare who is going to stand up and leap out of the barricades with all the corporals and privates behind him. This goes back in our country to even so moral a man as Abraham Lincoln. The story is told that while he was in the state legislature in Springfield, Illinois, a very controversial issue arose for a vote and he simply opened the window and jumped through it.

GORDON HOXIE: On that note, and with no suggestion that we jump either through windows or hoops, may I express our warm thanks to Dr. Gilmour and to a very distinguished panel in highlighting for the 70's domestic issue challenges.

CHAPTER IV

Foreign Policy for the 70's

GORDON HOXIE: *Introduction*

Our moderator, William J. Casey, Chairman of the Securities and Exchange Commission, was introduced as a member of the preceding round table on domestic policy. His expertise there has been vouched for. What is perhaps forgotten in his present post is that Mr. Casey has long been a student of American Foreign Policy and has distinguished himself most recently as a member of the General Advisory Committee, the United States Arms Control and Disarmament Agency. Last year here in our First National Leadership Symposium he brilliantly chaired the discussion on the formulation and implementation of American foreign policy.

Now it gives me pleasure to present an old friend appropriately moderating this overview of American Foreign Policy in the 1970's, the Honorable William J. Casey.

WILLIAM CASEY: Thank you, Gordon. Last year at this Symposium we traced the role of the President in foreign policy and the instrumentalities utilized in carrying out that role. By contrast with domestic policy, the President has relatively great power in the foreign policy field. The panel on domestic policy pointed out this afternoon that he does not have the same dominant leadership in that area as he has in foreign policy. Today, however, increasingly the Congress is seeking to exercise control in foreign policy, control which it had wrested from President Wilson, only to have it taken back by President F.D. Roosevelt.

The National Security Council and other machinery which has been developed to carry out our foreign policy today works most effectively. Through it we are going through a period of great reassessment. We have come a long way since John Kennedy said in 1961 that we were prepared to pay any price and bear any burden to maintain freedom throughout the world. We have come to believe through the experience of the last ten years, and this is a view shared by public opinion in the United States, that our power does not reach as far as we thought it did. We have come to believe that it is not as important as we thought it was to know all and control all in all parts of the globe. Instead, we have come to espouse what is known as the Nixon Doctrine. It can be defined as the support of others in maintaining a global balance on somewhat the same basis that England maintained a European balance for three centuries; it may mean other things, and I will defer to those here on the panel who are better qualified than I to deal with just what the Nixon Doctrine means in terms of present and projected foreign policy.

Going beyond the Nixon Doctrine, the President has decided that the time has come to deal with the reality of 800 million Chinese on the Asiatic mainland. That delicate task is made the more complex by the potential China-Russia conflict. We do not know the precise extent to which this has played a role in the willingness of the Chinese to open up a dialogue with the United States. Going down a little further south to the Indian sub-continent, we see perhaps the greatest human tragedy which the world has seen since Hitler and the holocaust of the 1939-1945 period. There are today some six to eight million refugees leaving Pakistan and flooding into India.

On a broader scale, the question of the strategic balance between the United States and the Soviet Union is a matter that has to be of enormous, continuing concern to the Presidency; there is the uncomfortable fact that the Soviet Union has built up its missile and atomic weapon resources dramatically over the last four or five years while our strategic weaponry level remains relatively unchanged. What effect will this have on the prospect and the hope for an arms control agreement? And what of the concern that perhaps the Soviet build-up will attain not just parity but superiority in a relatively short period of time. Although we do have today enough capability to inflict irreparable harm and unacceptable damage on the Soviet Union, we have to be concerned if they achieve sufficient superiority whether they will be able to convert that superiority into diplomatic and bargaining leverage as we were able to do at the time of the Cuban Crisis of 1962.

Then there is the question of the naval balance around the world, the degree to which the Soviet Union has moved out into the seven seas. There is the concern that if the Suez Canal is opened up, whether the Soviet naval force in the Mediterranean will open up East Africa to the Soviets, out-flank Israel, out-flank the Arab world and the oil fields of the Middle East.

Then there is the dramatic defeat in the Senate yesterday of the aid program and the impact that that can have on the Nixon Doctrine. And finally, there are the very complicated, the very important problems that strike home at the economic welfare of all of us, the monetary and trade conflicts which have prevailed for some time and which came to a boiling point in the last couple of months.

In brief, those are the things we are concerned about when we think about the American foreign policy in the 70's. To deal with them as we indicated last year, we have a greatly strengthened White House machinery to assist the President. There is concern and discussion as to what the proper relationship should be between the National Security Council and the Department of State. We are told that President John F. Kennedy and McGeorge Bundy, his National Security Affairs Advisor, used to dream that perhaps they could have a National Security Council of 40 or 50 and let the State Department drift out to sea, conducting foreign policy from the White House. Today we have a National Security staff of two and one half times that size.

One of the real problems of the Presidency is the difficulty of managing the national security and foreign policy machinery outside of the White House. Here I am not just talking about the State Department. We have the Central Intelligence Agency, which is larger than the State Department; we have the Agency for International Development, which is larger than the State Department; we have the United States Information Agency which is all over the world, almost 25 to 30 percent as big as the State Department; we have the Department of Defense representatives in the embassies around the world. There are more Defense representatives in the embassies around the world than our State Department representatives! There is a "little state department" over at the Pentagon headed by the Assistant Secretary of State for International Security Affairs; his former senior deputy is with us on this panel. Such organizations do tend to feed on each other. For example, the State Department a few years ago created a staff of about one hundred people to deal with the "little foreign office," over in the Pentagon. And this does tend to create layer upon layer of machinery.

It takes something like 20 people to clear a cable in the State Department, I am told. Then they have to clear these messages and these decisions with the other elements in the national foreign policy, national security machinery. And when there are conflicts between these units, Defense, CIA, AID, USIA, Peace Corps—very frequently only the President himself can resolve these conflicts.

Thus, increasingly, there is a feeling that if we are going to get command of the foreign policy machinery and execute and carry out a sensible foreign policy in the 70's, this machinery somehow has to be pared down to make it increasingly effective. Moreover, we have to reduce American presence in countries around the world. This is part of the Nixon Doctrine. We have had a series of studies, reports which have pointed out the need to accomplish this: The Fitzhugh Report on the Pentagon, the Peterson Report on foreign aid, the study with Secretary Melvin Laird which the White House has conducted on the intelligence machinery. In sheer numbers and sheer cost intelligence is the largest of all the segments of the American foreign policy machinery.

With that background, I am going to pass the discussion on to Richard A. Ware who in 1969-70 served with distinction as the Principal Deputy Assistant Secretary of Defense for International Security Affairs.

RICHARD A. WARE: Bill, I feel a bit inadequate talking about foreign policies because the Secretary of Defense told me on many many occasions that foreign policy is made by the Department of State, not the Department of Defense! And that reminds me of one of the late Alfred E. Smith's campaigns for governor of this State. It was in the middle of the speech that some fellow stood up, waved his arms, and said, "Tell 'em all you know, Al; it won't take long." And Al Smith replied immediately, "Let's both tell 'em; it won't take any longer!"

Now, I do not want particularly to deal with the structure of national security and foreign policy as it is determined within the Government, but I would like to point out a few of what I think are the key problems that the current President, or any President, has got to confront during the decade of the 70's.

There has been, I believe, under President Nixon, an historic change in United States foreign policy, perhaps the first major change since the days of Woodrow Wilson. The Nixon Doctrine is telling the world that we no longer, we the United States, are no longer going to be the policeman of the world. It further states that this function, this role, has to be performed by others in concert with us, at least to a much greater degree than in the past.

Last evening Jim Hagerty made the statement that one of the duties of the Presidency is to be the diplomatic leader of the free world. President Nixon made a speech in Kansas City not too long ago that has escaped attention. In that he made this comment, "Many of you are old enough to remember what America was 25 years ago. We were number one in the world militarily, with no one who even challenged us, because we had a monopoly of atomic weapons. Now, 25 years having passed, we see five great economic superpowers: The United States, Western Europe, the Soviet Union, China and, of course, Japan."

This says much in terms of what U.S. foreign policy will have to be and the issues it will have to confront in the decade that we have entered. The President chose to initiate our new role with the Nixon Doctrine, stated on Guam, to pass over to our allies much of the responsibility for their own defense and for the defense of that part of the world in which they are located. The problem of obtaining this kind of back-up support from our allies is a difficult one because over the years they have become reasonably spoiled and have coasted upon our backs.

It raises serious questions in the Pacific, for example, as to the future role of Japan, the question as to whether or not Japan for evermore can be considered a friend and ally of the United States. After all, twice in a century it reversed course 180°. This kind of a problem must be reckoned with. We have the new policy toward China, and its impact upon our relations with Japan. The strains resulting from the economic situation existing between Japan and the United States are further compounded by the vote in the United Nations General Assembly, where we carried Japan with us; now Japan suffers the loss of face in the Orient as having been associated with a whopping defeat. This is not going to make it easier for us to handle the defense problems of the western Pacific under the Nixon Doctrine.

Such problems are further compounded by what happened in

the Senate yesterday in terms of foreign aid—and I speak now from the standpoint primarily of military assistance. Recently we withdrew approximately 20,000 troops from Korea; we did it with a promise to the Republic of Korea that we would beef up their own armed forces. The wherewithal to do that, of course, is dependent upon the appropriations of the Congress. So part of the question here is the credibility of the Nixon Doctrine and of the President.

The problems of the Nixon Doctrine in Europe are every bit as serious and complicated by the Soviets looking over our shoulders. We must remember that as of today we have many more troops in Europe than we have in South Vietnam, and the pressure to withdraw those troops is going to increase. We have already seen some of the action in Congress on this issue. The credibility of the Nixon Doctrine as applied to Europe and European defense again is going to become of enormous importance.

I think that there is a third item of especial concern. Our strategy over the last 25 years has always been based upon strategic or nuclear superiority. We are at least entering a period of parity, if not something worse, depending on how you look at it. The question then comes as to what should our posture and policy be in a period of nuclear parity or inferiority. And where does this leave us and how do we manage our defense assets at a time when those assets are constantly being diminished? This is a serious question to which, I believe, we must address ourselves.

Related somewhat to this, also a practice of the last quarter century, is the policy of depending heavily upon a special relationship with the United Kingdom; a bit of a throwback to the days when the United Kingdom had more economic and military power than it does today. Today, with an insurgency within its own borders in Northern Ireland, one may well ask whether the United States can depend upon the United Kingdom in the future, over the next 25 years, as the keystone or linchpin to our relationships to the defense of Europe.

Then there is the impact of the British decision to become part of the Common Market, or really of another economic, political and, possibly military power. In other words, the Atlantic community is changing its situation, substantially.

I am impressed with a comment that Frank J. Shakespeare, Jr., Director of USIA, made several weeks ago in New York about the dimensions of determining foreign policy. In effect he said that in the period up until the Vietnam experience, i.e. in the period through the Korean incident and the decade of the 1950's, foreign policy rested quite substantially upon economic and military power; that these were the two major factors taken into consideration in structuring foreign policy. Vietnam, according to Frank Shakespeare, and I agree with him, has added a new dimension to this, and that is the instant communication that takes place. Now with television, in living color, instantaneously transmitting into the homes of our country, at the dinner hour, the scenes of combat, we have the whole population of this country being brought into the picture in a way that never occurred before in the determination of foreign policy in the councils of any government. If our foreign policy were ever determined by a political or leadership elite, I would submit I do not think it is true any longer.

In the long range view and on a related subject I have substantial doubt as to the wisdom of diplomacy conducted by heads of state, in direct relationship with other heads of state, sometimes referred to as "summit diplomacy." This first came to my attention some years ago when I read a very interesting little book called *The Ordeal of Woodrow Wilson*, written by Herbert Hoover. This is, I believe, the only book by an ex-President about an ex-President. It is a fascinating story of the problems that Wilson encountered when he attempted to negotiate a settlement following World War I. I believe Mr. Hoover made the observation prior to Mr. Wilson's going to Europe that an American President, when he leaves the country, does not carry with him the power that the head of a cabinet government, for example, carries. He cannot speak for Congress; Mr. Wilson learned this. He sometimes is encouraged to believe that he can by the greetings he receives from the peoples of foreign countries. In other words, he can fall victim to adulation. Lastly, he has lost some of the mystique of his office when he meets on that face-to-face basis. Some of the mystery of the White House, some of the illusions and mythology that are associated with political power tend to disappear. This type of a problem is brought out in this book.

W. Averell Harriman raises the same question in slightly different terms. He rather recently stated that the idea that the heads of government can go to another country and negotiate in a few days very complicated, and previously unexplored, in-depth issues, is really an unreality. The dangers inherent are that you put in all of your reserves. There is not anybody the President can refer to. On a matter of "yes" or "no" a lesser offi-cial could delay by saying he had to refer to his government, but with the heads of government there is no one in the background.

The late Dean Acheson put it a little bit differently, more pun-gently, as he was apt to when he kind of tweeked his mustache, stating, "When a chief of state, or head of government, makes a fumble in a direct negotiation with another head of state, the goal line is open behind him."

Let me finish up with a question. I think perhaps this is the key question confronting the current President. Can a major power, such as the United States, stand down and still continue to exert world-wide influence, especially when other countries know that the South Vietnamese experience has soured the taste of the U.S. population for overseas military involvement? This, I believe, is the dilemma that we confront in determining for-eign policy during the '70's.

WILLIAM CASEY: Thank you, Dick, for that thought provok-ing statement.

Our next speaker, as in the case of Mr. Ware, needs no intro-duction to the Center for the Study of the Presidency. We have made reference to our first National Leadership Symposium on the Presidency here in early April 1970. All of us were impressed by the cogent view on the occasion of Senior Staff Member of the National Security Council, Helmut Sonnenfeldt, and it is a plea-sure to welcome him back.

HELMUT SONNENFELDT: Thank you, Bill. It is good to be back as it is also to participate in the Center's Round Table dis-cussions in New York City. Last year here at Montauk we talked a bit about the structure of the National Security Council staff and its operations. The very excellent book that Gordon Hoxie put out as a result of that is available to all of you. Thus unless you have further questions, I think I will not repeat that part of the discussion.

Let me pick up the question of summit diplomacy that Dick Ware just referred to. I think that this President was perhaps as cautious about that particular device of diplomacy, a very dramatic and in some respects conclusive device of diplomacy, as any of his predecessors. Indeed, in terms of laying a firm foundation he has been more cautious than most. He was very conscious of the experiences in the Eisenhower Administration with the abortive summit with the Soviet Union that had been planned for the spring of 1960. He was conscious of the problems that arose in the Kennedy Administration with the Vienna meeting. He was conscious of the difficulties that arose more recently in the planning of summit meetings in the Johnson Administration.

I think we do have to realize, and this goes back to the reference to what Frank Shakespeare had to say, that in this modern era of rapid communication and rapid transportation there is enormous pressure on heads of government to enter into direct and frequent communication with their partners or with their opposite numbers in other countries. It has become physically easier to come together. Therefore, when a particularly dramatic moment arises the temptation for a summit meeting is undoubtedly greater than it was before. But this President is conscious of the problems both of the abortive efforts at summit diplomacy and of the pitfalls that Dean Acheson and others had talked about, that is to say that a President has no one that he can say that he wants to refer the question to as any ambassador or delegate can do.

Insofar as summitry for the Soviets is concerned, this President resisted enormous pressures right from the beginning of this term, right from the moment of inauguration, to become involved in summit diplomacy. Very early, I think at his first press conference, he established the principle that he would engage in this type of diplomacy with the Soviet Union, with the Soviet leadership, only when there has been sufficient progress in negotiations and relations at lower levels in the various areas so that a summit meeting, when it does occur, can have some promise of some concrete achievement. He was criticized for this at the time, particularly in connection with the delay in the opening of strategic arms talks which some people felt should be given the momentum, the impetus, of direct presidential involvement.

President Nixon held out for all this time in order to get the preliminaries established as clearly as possible before embarking on what is, admittedly, far from a riskless venture in so far as dealings with the Soviets are concerned. I do not believe, particularly after last night with congressional failure to support foreign aid, that this President is going to be under any illusion that he can speak for the Congress when he goes to Moscow.

Mr. Herbert Hoover, as Dick Ware noted, referred to the mystique of the Presidency that somehow will be tarnished or lost when the President moves abroad and is seen face-to-face and in some other mortal's office. My experience with Presidential travel has been that the mystique comes nowhere near the reality. I think that the people of Peking and the people of Moscow will not have lived until they have seen the presidential entourage arrive in Peking and Moscow. Bob Ginsburgh [Major General Robert N.], who is with us this weekend, may have had some similar experience of this sort when he served with President Johnson. In brief, I am not sure whether Mr. Hoover's point about the mystique stands up under the modern day Presidential traveling circus.

Now, we can come back, perhaps, to the projected China trip and the projected Moscow summit and any of the related subjects in the discussion period.

The key issue that this Presidency, this Administration, has had to confront, that a Humphrey Administration would have had to confront had Senator Humphrey been elected in 1968, is the change in the power balance and the power structure. The fact of the matter is that by 1968-1969, a great many forces that have determined international relations in the post-war period, had begun to undergo drastic change, and any President would have had to confront them. You are all aware of them; they involve such things as the change in the military balance, the proliferation of power and influence among several centers in the world instead of perhaps only the two that one had become accustomed to, the undermining of the old economic structures and the formation of new international economic structures that have come into existence essentially after World War II. Additionally, there is the very fundamental change in the nature of the Communist world; what was essentially a monolithic, or if not monolithic at least highly hierarchical grouping of states, has been transformed into a much more diffuse and diversified grouping including the deep-seated animosities and antagonisms between the two major parties in the Communist world.

And then in Europe there is the revitalization, the psychological rebirth, of the Europeans, the gradual movement toward European economic unity—something we had advocated over the years in the 50's but had not ever really thought about very seriously in terms of its effect upon us when and as it succeeded. This was something that was confronting us in the late 60's.

All of these things have been compounded by the domestic attitudes that have been alluded to. Any President, therefore, had the task of adjusting, of attempting to adjust, the American role in the world to this accumulation of frequently contradictory new forces, of changing forces that impinge on international politics, and adjusting it as well to the changing attitude of Americans.

I do not, myself, think that the image of the United States as the policeman of the world is one that is particularly consonant with our history, although it is a function that the United States performed in much of the post-World War II era. But the United States, in its relationship to the outside world, has gone through a certain cycle which, however, has some common features. To use a very gross and crass shorthand, up until World War I Americans essentially thought of themselves as too good to involve themselves in the messy affairs of the outside world and wanted to stay aloof from the world. There was a sense of innocence about the American experience, a sense of idealism about the American experience, shared, incidentally, by many persons from foreign shores who looked longingly at the United States. This is evidenced by the flood of immigrants who came to pre-1914 America.

Then Mr. Wilson's crusade to make the world safe for democracy was followed by a decade of disillusionment, disenchantment, and again withdrawal from active leadership in world affairs other than in humanitarian activities. Despite the efforts of the dynamic President Franklin Roosevelt, it took the events of December 7, 1941, Pearl Harbor, to bring the United States to full involvement in World War II.

We fought strenuously and effectively in World War II and then conducted our policies in the post-war period in a way that would make the world more like us. That is to say, where before we would not join the world because it was not enough like us, we decided in World War II and in the post-World War II period that if we had to join it, we had better make it as much like us as we could. A great many of our policies had this particular thread running through them.

Now, in the most recent period, many of the people that were involved in this highly idealistic, and often extremely devoted, service to world improvement, of spreading an umbrella of security over a threatened world, began to be caught up in the sense of overcommitment. This often took the form of a deep sense of guilt about American involvement in the affairs of other countries. And, whereas in the earlier period, we had thought ourselves too good to be part of the world, many of our people came to think of us as too bad to be part of the world. And this is, of course, a manifestation that we have witnessed, particularly among many of our young people and a large segment of our intellectual community.

In brief, the psychological underpinning for American involvement in the world has become very complex and very difficult. And a President can no longer, in the 1970's, at least in the early 1970's, count on the idealism and the devotion that made American involvement possible in the previous periods. On the contrary, he now encounters hostility, resistance, withdrawal and guilt.

The problem obviously has no easy solution. Moreover, the concern about excessive involvement, about excessive commitments, about excessive expenditures of resources extends beyond the intellectual and the youth groups that I was referring to. There are, after all, a great many more conservatively inclined groups in our society who always have questions about the degree of American involvement in world affairs. Indeed, in the 40's and 50's there had been a certain merging of those doubts and that skepticism with the more virulent kinds of doubts in the other portions of our society.

So the consensus behind any international-minded policies is now a very shaky and very thin consensus. What this Administration has attempted to do, and I believe what in a different style and a different way another administration might have attempted to do as well, is this: it has sought to face the reality that the United States, by virtue of its size and by virtue of the kind of world that we live in, the shrinking world we live in, cannot realistically expect to turn its back upon the world altogether. This Administration has sought to do this living in the world as we do and at the same time as being consistent as we possibly can with what Americans in the 70's will psychologically and emotionally bear in the way of the burdens of involvement.

Now that is more easily said than done; it has to be translated into specific day-to-day policies. But that is essentially the problem that this President has had to face. These considerations should be taken into account in any assessment of the powers of the Presidency and the size of the White House staff and the White House operation. Indeed, these considerations along with all these other attitudes having to do with our international involvements, with our priorities, have made more complex the capacity and the task of Presidential leadership.

The experience of 1968, of President Johnson renouncing the possibility of another term under the conditions that he did, that experience does not obviously enhance the power of the Presidency. Now this is a problem for all of us: whatever the precise balance between the President and Congress—and one can clearly argue about that—this system of government depends upon a strong and vigorous Presidency.

So this President, or another President, had he been elected, had to face the problem of guiding the country into this period of very substantial adjustment in the face of new international conditions and in the face of changing moods at home. President Nixon had to face that problem under conditions where the Presidency, itself, was in some degree of crisis; and that has also been the task of this President: to cope with and correct over the last three years many of the things Jim Hagerty and George Reedy alluded to last evening and George referred to in his book *Twilight of the Presidency*. You may recall that this volume first appeared in our conference here last year and Gordon Hoxie on that occasion expressed the hope that twilight might rather be dawn.

WILLIAM CASEY: Thank you Hal. While you advisedly stayed away from matters of foreign policy structure, what observations can you offer about a foreign policy establishment which has come to encompass 100,000 persons in several headquarters in Washington and floating around the world? Some of these are working independent channels of command. In reality, however, all of the important decisions get brought into the White House and get worked out by a relatively small staff. Now what kind of problems of co-ordination does this create? Will this huge foreign policy establishment gravitate more and more to White House control? Where do you think that establishment can go? What do you think can happen to it over the decade of the 70's.

HELMUT SONNENFELDT: First of all, the decision-making process, of course, is highly centered on the President, and that does ultimately mean that major decisions tend to be made at the top of the pyramid. Then there is the problem of coordinating Cabinet level matters. The only place where such matters can be resolved is the President, or the President in Council as Gordon Gray referred to it here last year. If a decision of magnitude is not resolved, this becomes a decision in and of itself. It usually means that action goes either in the direction of one or the other of the contestants.

In fact, it is a common frustration of Presidents, that a great many decisions still continue to be made in the agencies that commit the President to courses of action that he has not necessarily himself approved. It is a constant problem that Presidents find themselves in. Even though it appears that every decision is made in the White House, Presidents constantly complain that far too many decisions are made all over the place, by action or inaction, which gives their administration—that is not markedly different in this Administration from other administrations—a particular coloration, a particular direction that is not the intended one of the President.

So, I do not think that this present system is excessively conducive to having inconsequential decisions made in the White House or by the Presidency, or by the President personally. I think by and large the rule of thumb is that if an issue is sufficiently important that it engages the prestige and resources, the intellectual resources, and the other resources of contesting elements in the bureaucracy, there is almost no way in which you can avoid having this in some way resolved in the White House. Now the council and staff mechanism in this Administration, including the new Domestic Council paralleling the National Security Council, was set up to try and make this a more systematic process than had been the case in some previous administrations. The goal is to anticipate the issues, by getting the positions of the different agencies—and even within different agencies—out on the table. The method is to have all the advantages and disadvantages of a given approach to a problem clearly laid out and debated openly and gotten up to the President in that form.

This President has perhaps made it harder for himself than past Presidents by insisting that he does not want to have consensus decisions come up to him from the agencies where he only has a choice of saying either yes or no; he has insisted on being given the elements of the problem and the options that he has for dealing with it; and then selecting the option himself. This is a very tough and exacting job. And that is one of the reasons why there perhaps is more staff in this Presidency than there was in the previous Presidency.

In the Eisenhower Administration, by contrast, a staff system with position papers was used; policy papers that came to the President were papers that had been negotiated below the Presidency, frequently involving "lowest common denominator" decisions. This was not always the case, but frequently. Jim Hagerty who is here may want to amplify or correct or contradict this, but the President was essentially faced with a choice of saying "approve" or "disapprove."

That is not the approach in this Presidency where a staff system is used but the decisions are made by the President himself. Now, a large part of the numbers of people in the agencies, are people that have to be concerned with implementing rather than deciding or defining policies. That frequently takes manpower. On the other hand, where no programs of substantial substance are involved, that is, where money is *not* being allocated, and where only the traditional tasks of diplomacy are being performed—contacts with governments, negotiations with governments—that manpower has been drastically cut.

Thus, as Dick Ware pointed out, in our embassies abroad today, the State Department component is normally the smallest. The largest staffs in most embassies are those that administer programs, and in some instances people concerned with military and other esoteric activities. But the State Department part of the personnel structure is increasingly declining both in Washington and abroad.

WILLIAM CASEY: Turning from Mr. Sonnenfeldt's review of policy formulation and implementation, I am going to ask Deputy Undersecretary of the Navy, Joseph A. Grimes, Jr., to tell us how this decision-making process looks from the other end of the spectrum.

JOSEPH A. GRIMES, JR.: Thank you. Mr. Ware and Mr. Sonnenfeldt have dealt principally with the substance of our foreign policies in the 70's. I would like to focus on the decision-making implementation of those policies. I think it was Hal last year at this conference who said that a President is not a great President only if he makes good decisions; he must also effectively implement them. And earlier in this conference, George Reedy was pointing out that the power of a President depends to a great extent on his ability to communicate with the people of the country, to get them behind his leadership and the policies that he espouses.

This is true not only for the country at large, but for the bureaucracy—the people that have to implement the policies that the President decides upon. First of all, they must believe in the policy to execute it fully and faithfully. Secondly they must believe that the President believes in it.

In an earlier incarnation I worked in the foreign aid program in Latin America, and I especially remember the years 1966 and 1967. President Johnson made some speeches about the great importance of Latin America. There was, he said, no place more important to the United States. At the same time, Alliance for Progress appropriations were being cut, and more and more A.I.D. people were being sent to Vietnam. As a result, the people in A.I.D. working on the Alliance for Progress simply did not believe him.

The question of leadership can also be illustrated by looking at the Defense Department. There were great innovations put in by Robert McNamara, but the military felt that they were not participating, or even being listened to. One of the great accomplishments of Melvin Laird, I believe, is that he has made the military feel that he values their opinions. It is ironic that under Mr. McNamara the defense budget increased significantly, and yet the military felt that they had never been listened to less. Under Mr. Laird, we have made a substantial cutback in defense spending, in relation to the gross national product; it is the lowest percentage of the gross national product in 20 years. Yet the military people feel that they are at least participating in decision-making.

I think the present set up of the NSC, the way the President uses it, has been quite effective along this line. There has been a gradual build-up to changes, for example, the Nixon Doctrine. That new direction in foreign policy had been discussed in general terms for quite some time before the President articulated his views on Guam. Because of this background it was no great surprise to anybody; it was not a sudden shift in direction. The same really is true of our "new" China policy. It was a surprise when President Nixon announced that Henry Kissinger had been to Peking and that he himself was going, but the elements of a change in policy had been coming; the harbingers were there. They were evident in the bureaucracy; they were evident in the country at large; and I think people were ready for it.

Another aspect of the decision-making implementation is what I would call "flexible response." Some people feel that when a President makes a decision, everybody has to make an immediate right turn. However, that is generally not the kind of decision the President makes, because he knows—or should know—that abrupt changes in direction can have surprising and undesirable ramifications that the President cannot foresee. Indeed, the bureaucracy has many new decisions of its own to make in response to a new policy, and properly so.

I will give you one example of a case where there was too much decision-making at the Presidential level. During the early days of the Alliance for Progress the constitutionally-elected government of Honduras was overthrown, and the word came out of the White House that all disbursements of loans would stop immediately. Unfortunately, some of these loans were to private banks that had been set up to encourage people to invest in their own country instead of sending their money abroad; other disbursements were to agricultural credit operations for small farmers who were just beginning to get their own land, their own seed, and their own tractors. So we wound up with a decision that went too far, too fast. The basic policy may have been sound, but the bureaucracy should have been given a little more time and flexibility to implement it.

Another point I would add is that decisions have to be made at all levels. The question is, where is the most appropriate place to make any given decision? I think it was Mr. Reedy who said earlier that unless a paper gets on the President's desk, it does not really count. Well, that just is not true. There are important decisions made all the way down the line. The role of the President should be to lead the bureaucracy, to make decisions that they believe in and to create a policy framework that guides the bureaucracy toward decisions consistent with the President's overall objectives. Sometimes, for specific purposes, he can come in and make decisions that he would not ordinarily make.

Let me give an example from this Administration. I will leave the country anonymous. The President was pushing for a reduction in the number of Americans stationed overseas, both military and civilian. This kind of objective takes time to accomplish and sometimes the bureaucracy is a little slow to respond. There is a tendency to figure out why they cannot do this; they have heard such objectives before, and often they question the strength of the President's commitment, sometimes with good reason. To overcome this bureaucratic inertia President Nixon issued an order that there would be a 25 percent personnel reduction in country "X" by such and such a date. Now, leaving aside whether the decision was right or wrong, this case illustrates how a President can "send a message" to the bureaucracy by inserting himself into the decision-making process at an unexpected point in time.

Some people have objected to the number of recommendations or decisions that are made at the National Security Council level. However, we are now going through a period of changing national values. The world is changing, and this means that many more decisions are going up to a higher level. The President has had the wisdom to remain somewhat vague on policies like the Nixon Doctrine or our future relationships with China. When new policies are not fully spelled out a significant number of decisions have to be sent to a higher level. I think that this will continue for several more years until a new consensus on foreign policy is reached.

Now, a little bit on the procedure involved in decision-making. I think it is very important for any organization to have a mechanism that can bring questions up for decision, preferably in the form of alternatives. This is very difficult to achieve in a bureaucracy, as the NSC staff well knows, because normally a course of action is presented to the decision-maker for approval or disapproval. In most cases a bureaucrat will seek to write his recommendations in such a way that the decision-maker can come to only one rational decision. I have a couple of aphorisms on this: Never give the boss an alternative; he may pick the wrong one. And if you have to give him one, make sure the one you do not want is totally unacceptable. Because of this danger of bureaucratic bias, every organization needs some independent group that has no axe to grind, and whose sole job is to take a look at all the options.

When a new organization is created, such as the National Aeronautics and Space Administration, it will take a fresh look at things; it wants to. So will a new team in an older organization. But we cannot rely on such fortuitous circumstances. Every organization, whether new like NASA or old like the Navy, must have a mechanism that can bring up innovative ideas in a dispassionate way. The same is true in the broader area of foreign affairs, and that is one of the reasons why the NSC was created. The nature of our relationships with other countries has drastically changed in the past thirty years, and the State Department is no longer so clearly *primus inter pares* among the federal departments and agencies that are active overseas. Not surprisingly this has caused some unhappiness in the ranks of our foreign service officers.

Former Ambassador Charles W. Yost wrote an article for this month's *Foreign Affairs* in which he nostalgically calls for a return to the good old days. Now a Professor at Columbia, he suggests that the NSC is a bad idea; that there is too much military influence and that we should go back to a system where the State Department runs things. I disagree. I think the world has changed too much for that.

The State Department has a built-in bias, just like every other department. It has a long history of diplomatic relationships with other countries. And that long history of being pretty much the only department dealing directly with other countries influences the way foreign service officers think. Yet in the past 25 to 30 years many federal agencies have greatly expanded their overseas operations, and their objectives often clash with the traditional diplomatic objectives of the State Department. Quite understandably none of those other agencies wants to have the final policy decision rest with an agency like State, which has its own institutional objectives.

Yes, the world has changed. Fifteen years ago, for example, we did not know the meaning of a balance of payments problem.

Today there are new economic powers in the world that did not exist 20 years ago, and because of that development we have a new and powerful player in the game—the Treasury Department.

Moreover, there are all kinds of domestic questions that impinge on the foreign policy area. There was a time when immigration was strictly a domestic concern; today it is very much of an international concern. The same is true of tariffs. Just look at the difference in approach to this problem between today and fifty years ago.

The most remarkable new international concern is the environment. In recent years the State Department has been having discussions with the NATO nations on oil spills, supposedly affecting only non-military ships. At the same time there have been international meetings on the environment, such as the forthcoming Stockholm Conference, and there have been negotiations on the law of the sea. More recently proposals have been made to create coastal state pollution-free zones which would permit the coastal states to monitor and inspect any ships going through their pollution-free zones, which in turn have become entangled with fishery zones and undersea exploitation rights.

As a result of these developments, all these little groups that have been meeting separately have found that their issues are very much interrelated with law of the sea discussions. When this happens, decisions are inevitably pushed to a higher level and properly so, because one department, such as State, cannot be given the power to make decisions affecting what other departments consider their vital interests.

One other subject worth mentioning is the question of checks and balances. Do these exist in the foreign policy area to the extent that they do in the domestic area, or is the President free to do anything he wants? Certainly he does not have the same constraints, but there are *a lot more* than many people like to admit. First of all, the amount that he can spend for military assistance and for foreign aid is very limited and the number of restrictions on the use of the money has increased over the years. Secondly, most of the programs in the foreign area have been thoroughly debated in this country. Just think back on the Marshall Plan. For the past twenty-five years the foreign aid program has been debated inside and out. We have heard about containment of Communism, winning friends abroad, humanitarian relief, and the building up of markets so that we can sell to foreign countries. How about the strategic deterrent? We have certainly heard plenty about massive retaliation, superiority, parity, sufficiency and all the other concepts for sizing our strategic forces.

The force levels in Europe have been debated many, many times and there are discussions in the Senate going on concerning this issue right now, including proposals that specific reductions take place. So also there is the matter of our role in Latin America, Africa, and the Eastern Mediterranean, to say nothing of Korea and Southeast Asia. All have been thoroughly debated in this country, and if the extent of public discussion means anything, then the President does not have the free hand some people think he has.

Finally, let me go back to the decision-making process. Carefully thought out procedures alone are not going to answer all our questions. But I think that these improved procedures that we now have will help us make more rational decisions. I hope so, because we need all the help we can get to make the right decisions in such a fast changing world.

WILLIAM CASEY: Thank you Secretary Grimes for your splendid contribution. Our next speaker is Dr. Hoxie's present military boss. Major General Robert N. Ginsburgh is one of the military's most distinguished students and practitioners of national security affairs. A Harvard Ph.D., a former Council on Foreign Relations Fellow, a former Senior Staff Member of the National Security Council, he is the author of a number of works on military strategy, General Ginsburgh.

ROBERT N. GINSBURGH: Thank you, Bill, and I am glad to have the identification with one of our hardworking reservists, Gordon Hoxie, who is also your Center President.

There have been several comments on the paucity of the State Department representation here. I will note in passing that I, too, like Hal Sonnenfeldt, am a refugee from the State Department. Unlike Hal, I am also a refugee, or perhaps an exile, from the National Security Council Staff. As a former member of the NSC staff, I would like to thoroughly endorse the present Administration's increase in the size of the NSC staff. For the two and a half years that I was there, I never got a day off, not even on a weekend, to attend a conference of this character!

Despite the very difficult nature of foreign policy issues and despite the variety of them, I suspect that Dr. David Haight was correct when he suggested this morning that providing we can maintain appropriate force and research and development levels the most significant problems in the 70's would be the domestic issues, plus those international policies having implications for domestic issues. I suspect that he is right, and I certainly hope that he is. I think it is important, however, that we not engage in wishful thinking, that we not assume that it will automatically be so, that we take the steps that are necessary to make it so. And I would say that the business of making it so is the number one foreign policy problem for the 70's.

Restating it, the major foreign policy problem for the 70's, it seems to me, is to cope with the foreign policy issues in a way that will enable us to devote the time and energy we will need to devote to some very key domestic issues. I think there is a certain parallel to what Mr. Casey said this afternoon when he pointed out that the success of our domestic programs will depend on a healthy economy. The parallel is that the success of our domestic programs also depends on the right kind of international environment.

I was especially interested to note last night from Mr. Hagerty's report that President Eisenhower considered one of the major accomplishments of his eight years in office the preservation of an adequate military force after a war for the first time in the history of the United States. Similarly, I would say that if the U.S. is to achieve its current domestic objectives President Nixon will also have to preserve adequate military force as this war in Vietnam draws to a close and thereafter.

May I hasten to point out that the adequacy of military force is *not* just a military question. It involves diplomatic, political, and economic issues as well. In large measure, I would suggest that the adequacy of any particular force level or any particular budgetary level for military forces will depend in the near future, and perhaps in the long range future, on the outcome of such things as: the President's trip to Peking and whatever agreements or consensus may come out of that; the President's trip to Moscow; the results of the SALT talks in Vienna and Helsinki; the international results of President Nixon's new economic program; the results of discussions, assuming they get underway, on the MBFR, that is the Mutual Balance Force Reduction; plus the true intentions and the capabilities of our potential adversaries.

Our challenge is to cope with these problems. Please note that I use the word *cope* rather than *solve;* we ought to talk about coping with problems rather than solving them because I do not think there are ultimate solutions for these complicated problems in foreign affairs.

Assuming that we can cope with these problems, through a well-coordinated foreign and national security policy, we should have a reasonable assurance of being able to continue to deter general war and hopefully somewhat better prospects than in the recent past in deterring smaller wars or finishing them quickly if it is in our interest, in our national interest, to fight them.

There will, nonetheless, remain a host of difficult foreign policy problems. But I would suggest that for the next decade, assuming we can take care of these others, that the interesting, the difficult ones, are more likely to be in the field of international economics.

Let me say just a brief word on Presidential decision-making. I would like to re-emphasize the distinctions made earlier by several speakers between the domestic and the foreign policy role of the President, and the different sets of constraints that the President works under. I do not think that there is any way of jiggering the system so that we can guarantee that the President is going to make the right decision. I do not think that the solution is to try to adopt techniques which are useful for domestic policy making; I do not think we ought to try to transfer those because I do not think they are transferable to the foreign policy field.

It does not seem to me that the proposal to publicly expose the divisiveness that may exist in a Presidential administration is the answer. And I take strong issue with some of George Reedy's remarks about the isolation of the President, the isolation especially of President Johnson. It seemed to me that the problem was not that he was isolated, but that he was listening to *too many different* voices, too many different voices within his own Administration, and that he was seeking to compromise fundamentally irreconcilable points of view. Now I think this is a useful approach toward legislation, toward domestic policy, but it is a tough way to provide foreign policy leadership. And it is a specially difficult way to try and fight a war.

I do not think we should try to impose changes on the institution of the Presidency; I do not think that is the answer. It seems to me that the way of working toward an answer is to be found basically in a way of increasing the Congressional role in foreign policy formulation, to find a way of increasing that role without diminishing the role of the President, to increase the Congressional participation in a responsible and a positive way.

This will require joint action on the part of the President and on the part of the Congress. It will require a mutual confidence between the President and the Congress, a confidence which has existed in some period in the past but which does not seem to exist at the moment. And finally, I would suggest this requires certain internal reforms within the Congress. These might, indeed, be the subject of a future symposium.

WILLIAM CASEY: Thank you, Bob, for that succinct statesmanlike statement.

GORDON HOXIE: In reading the record of this Symposium prior to its publication, I noted Bob Ginsburgh's generous reference to my role as an Air Force Reserve general officer. This, in turn, has inspired me to include at this point a synopsis of the speech delivered by Lieutenant General Glen W. Martin, Vice-Commander in Chief, Strategic Air Command, delivered at the USAF Reserve General Officer Conference in Denver, Colorado on 28 September 1972.

This is the first time that this Center has published in its Proceedings remarks not delivered in its own lectures and symposia. However, General Martin has so incisively pointed up what he considers "the most vital *security issue* of the Seventies," which complements our discussion on that subject, that I have exercised this prerogative as the volume's editor, with General Martin's gracious consent.

General Martin brings to a discussion of national security policy a rich background of experience. He was the Deputy Chief of Staff for Plans and Operations for the Air Force until 1970 and had earlier served as the military executive to the Secretary of the Air Force.

In including in this volume a summary of General Martin's

remarks, may I add it points up something of the rich opportunities for insights and perspectives in this area provided by the Air Force for its reserve general officers.

GLEN W. MARTIN: The most vital *security issue* of the Seventies is the *relationship* between the *strategic power* of the United States and that of the Soviet Union. Over the past decade the Soviet Union has pursued a course toward nuclear superiority. I believe a major catalyst for this advancement was the United States' strategic concept of "assured destruction."

The original policy called for a strategic force which could inflict unacceptable damage on an aggressor, after absorbing that aggressor's surprise attack. This rationale influenced a leveling off of our ICBM and SLBMs and a decline in our number of bombers.

There are several critical weaknesses in the assured destruction philosophy. First, it is dangerous to entrust our security to a theoretical assumption of what damage might be unacceptable to an aggressor. Further, a narrowly focused strategic force could be overtaken by technological surprise before our counter efforts could be effective. Finally, an assured destruction capacity by itself limits the options available for dealing with less than all out war.

The President has recognized this fallacy and has defined a new posture which he calls "strategic sufficiency" or "forces adequate to prevent us and our allies from being coerced." The Secretary of Defense has enunciated the corollary strategy of realistic deterrence. It is our duty in the military to support that policy and to recommend the means to achieve it.

Today we find ourselves in a position of numerical inferiority in some areas and if the Soviets were to gain a technological lead they could have clear strategic superiority. Such a shift would place in Soviet hands the most powerful instrument for negotiation and coercion in the nuclear age. That is the major danger of the Seventies which we must be alert to and guard against.

A look at Soviet actions since World War II may offer a clue to potential problems in the Seventies. The immediate post World War II years were the Soviet expansion years in Europe. The countries of Eastern Europe were integrated into the Soviet camp. These included Poland, Rumania, Bulgaria, Czechoslovakia and East Germany.

In 1950 the Soviets attempted further expansion of Communism in Korea. They then moved into the uncommitted countries of Asia, the Middle East and Africa.

The Sixties began with the Soviets testing the strength of the West in Berlin. Then in 1962 Khrushchev attempted to establish a strategic missile base in Cuba. We called that bluff, and the Soviets were forced to withdraw the missiles. The key factor was our overwhelming strategic superiority.

The major lesson of that historical confrontation is the overriding importance of a strategic force of sufficient strength in resolving a crisis. The key of a continued credible deterrent force for the coming decade will be the effective modernization of our strategic TRIAD, [i.e. the bomber and both the land based and the submarine launched ballistic missile forces].

The B-52 has for many years been the backbone of the U. S. bomber force. But, improvements will be needed to insure that it can compete effectively against an ever improving Soviet defensive structure. The new B-1 will be needed to modernize the bomber as a continuing part of our TRIAD into the 1980's.

The cornerstone of our strategic retaliatory posture is the MINUTEMAN force of 1000 missiles. Concurrently, MINUTEMAN III is replacing the older MINUTEMAN I missiles. Further modernization of our ICBMs will depend on continuing technological improvements.

Modernization of the submarine launched ballistic missile force, improved reconnaissance, increased aerial refueling capacity and strengthened defensive structure will also be vital to a credible deterrent posture in the Seventies. A viable reserve force for immediate augmentation of the active Air Force is also essential, especially in the era of an all volunteer force.

We should not ignore the lessons of the past. We must not allow the hope of peace to cloud our judgment of reality. The President made the point when he said: "A strong America is not the enemy of peace. It is the guardian of peace."

WILLIAM CASEY: Our next panelist came to the Department of State 30 years ago, after receiving his Ph.D. degree from the Fletcher School of Law and Diplomacy. He has been with the department ever since with the exception of service in the Navy in World War II. He has been Director of the Historical Office since 1962 and was the recipient of the Department's Meritorius Service Award in 1963. Dr. Franklin, as an historian, can you comment on these matters of proliferation of foreign policy organization?

WILLIAM FRANKLIN: Particularly after these very thoughtful discussions and in view of the complex problems of the relation of the Department with the other agencies of Government in the 70's ahead, I do not believe I should focus on matters of organization in the few minutes alloted.

But let me as a late addition to your panel speak instead as an historian. References have been made to summit meetings; this is important particularly for the Center for the Study of the Presidency. But summit meetings have been with us a long time, and those at the summit have a fatal fascination for them and have had for a long time. History shows well back into the age of kings that such meetings have often served a very useful purpose.

Now, I am aware as a student of Government of the pitfalls that were pointed out by Mr. Ware, that Presidents have to be watched; let me say that dictators and kings have had to be watched even more closely! But the fact is that heads of state at the summit often get things done in a hurry, which would otherwise not get done at all. The experience in World War II provides a classic case in point. Whatever the post-war decisions may have been, Churchill, Roosevelt, and Stalin organized the largest military operations in history. Some of their conferences then served a very real and effective purpose. I am sure Molotov must have whispered to Stalin from time to time: you know if you can get to Roosevelt, maybe you can get some decisions made. In retrospect some of Roosevelt's critics believed too many decisions were made. The point is that they were made by virtue of the meeting at the summit.

At the end of World War II the prestige of the United States was unchallenged. The historian may well ask how in the past 25 years has that prestige diminished. Was it lost in summit meetings or was it lost in the national will? Before seeking to plot any new courses for the 70's we might well reflect upon the national purpose, the national determination. What brought about this loss of prestige. What brought our travail of the 60's?

Perhaps one is most struck if you look back over a larger period of American history, at our loss of prestige abroad. In general, we do not any more represent that *ideal* that the United States grew great on abroad. We have more power than ever before, but less prestige. It has been said that the United States for generations exerted a profound influence not so much as a nation but rather as an idea; it was the idea of social organization represented by the Statue of Liberty, viewed as very real throughout the world. We represented certain standards and certain values which carried tremendous weight, even during periods of American isolation and physical weakness.

The historian might be tempted to note we have come out of isolation and into greater participation with greater force than ever before, but somehow some of that idealism seems to have been lost along the way. If some of this can be regained in the 70's, less force would be necessary for American leadership to be effective throughout the world.

WILLIAM CASEY: Dr. Franklin, we thank you for that penetrating philosophical statement. We believe that the Department of State has been well represented here this evening!

Let us take comments or questions now. I see the hand of a professor from Fairleigh Dickinson University.

BRUTUS COSTE: We have heard three panels in large part discussing foreign policy. The first one, last evening, told us that each President, beginning with Eisenhower in 1953 and ending with the present occupant of the White House, has faced different problems. As Mr. Hagerty expressed it, each has done as well as could be expected in the circumstances. What we have looked for is how did it happen that, whereas at the end of the Eisenhower Administration the preponderence of power was on this side, such no longer obtains. Somehow everybody seems to have done well; yet the outcome is not something one can be very happy about. What is the explanation? Is there some fatalism involved or is human error involved?

Then we come to the second area of discussion on foreign affairs which we heard here this morning, that was about what information should be made available to the people of this country in order for them to make intelligent decisions. It seems to me that there again the main point was missed because what was important is not so much how much information you release as it is how correct your perception is and how correct a perception you transmit to the people.

Now, I can remember that at a time when American power was overwhelming, in the 50's, the people of the United States and of the western world were talking in terms of containing Russia, when the reality was the other way around. The Soviet Union was containing the superior power of the western world. Then again, in the late 50's when the power equation was at its best, the main concern of the western world was about this strange idea that the fate of the world could be decided by the weak and powerless uncommitted nations; that everything was a matter of health and economic assistance.

And so the question seems to be this: was not the real problem, through most of the past years, the absence of a perceptive appraisal of the true facts of world politics? It appears that instead of facing problems, we were shoving them under the carpet. They were bound to kick back sometime in the future. And they began to do so in the late 1960's to the extent that Mr. Johnson did not run for re-election.

And I come to this evening's panel. I have heard very interesting things about the methods by which foreign policy decisions are made. But we are being entertained with false optimism; we are being told that we have the chance, for the first time since the end of World War II, to come near to a generation of peace. But the facts of the situation do not confirm this optimism. We delude ourselves with the idea of the disintegration of our opponent, when, in fact, we are witnessing the disintegration of our own camp.

So let me conclude by saying I would be happier if I had been given this impression that it is somewhere between 11:55 and 12:05. No one of us can say with any precision where we are today. I want to hope that it is not too late; it can be too late if there is no awakening and we continue to generate complacency, i.e. if we fail to face up to the worst. Thank you.

WILLIAM CASEY: I think that is a very valuable contribution to the discussion. When you ask how we got where we are, I would say, in a nutshell, we got where we are because of foreign policy mistakes and misassessments as to where we should put our resources, where we committed them. The abysmal strategy of the Vietnamese thing really sapped the will of the American people, sapped their will to face the realities which may be in the world as you see them.

116

Now, I think the most critical and meaningful part of the discussion that we have had is what to do about that. And Mr. Sonnenfeldt addressed himself to it and addressed himself to it in terms of the limitations placed upon the President, the fact that the American people are not ready to support and not ready to face some of the dangers that may exist in the world. And I was somewhat disappointed in the discussion, too, because it seemed to me that the really important thing is what has to be done, what can be done to alert and educate the American people to the risks and the perils that may exist in the world as you see it. Moreover, how are we to revive this weakened will which, I agree, has over-taken the public spirit in this country. Now, Hal, do you have anything to add to that?

HELMUT SONNENFELDT: No, I welcome your contribution as well though it is 11:20, so I think possibly we have a little more time for a variety of reasons. There are two things that I would say, and that I think all of us ought to be clear about. First, there is the fact that the overwhelming physical strength that the United States commanded in the aftermath of the war was an atypical situation; it could not have been realistic for us to expect to maintain that sort of monopoly of physical power. There was no physical way in which the United States could prevent the Soviet Union, unless we were to be entirely contradictory to all our traditions and values, from acquiring a certain military capacity with which to damage the United States. I think to that degree there is a certain inevitability about it; there is nothing that we could have done to prevent the Soviet Union from building certain numbers of ICBM's and so on and so forth.

I do think that perhaps there occurred errors in judgment in the kind of military forces that we ourselves acquired. There is no doubt that the way the Vietnam War was fought affected the mood and the will, the values and the priorities, in this country the way that Mr. Casey suggested. And we are in a situation where we have to retrieve our poise and our composure to do the things that we have to do. At the same time I think that we will have to face the fact that we cannot ever again expect to conduct our affairs with a kind of physical security that we enjoyed during the era of our nuclear monopoly. There is no way in which that can be restored. And it seems to me to look for ghosts under

117

the bed in an effort to repeal what has happened is going to mislead us and lead us astray from the task before us.

The other comment that I would make is that we do have serious problems in our camp, as you call it; we do have serious problems at home. I think, again, we would make a mistake if we continue to assume that in the Communist world there are not divergences, differences, fissures and opportunities for the United States and other countries to advance and pursue their interests. Those things do exist, and I think one of the things in this Administration has been a cautious, but nevertheless purposeful effort to take account of the diversities that do exist in the Communist world.

Those things I would say in qualification of what you have said, but I would not for a minute deny that the problems that we face around the world, the dangers that we face around the world, the fact that we are not operating in a situation of physical safety and certainly not in a situation of physical superiority, that this does pose the most serious problems for us at a time when a large portion of our population does not even recognize that that is a problem.

RICHARD WARE: Let me just add to what Hal has said. I think one of the enormous contributions of President Nixon, Secretary Laird, Secretary Rogers, Henry Kissinger, indeed all those involved in determining national strategy policy during these difficult days, has been to manage a diminishing defense storehouse of assets in a way that has not put us in a more serious bind, given the situation that we confront within the country domestically.

Whenever the Defense Department sought more money or tried to prevent certain draw-downs in our force structure, I do not recall any group of citizens coming to our assistance on Capitol Hill. And the reality, politically, of the situation in this country is that you have to have the support of the people for what you are doing. We have not had that support. The Defense Department has been under attack; the uniformed military has been downgraded in the eyes of the public. And until we recover from this situation and have public support for viable defense policies, we are not going to have them, no matter what the power of the Presidency or the Secretary of Defense.

Where is the outcry, where is the outpouring of interest in

the decision of the Senate yesterday to negate foreign aid. Here was an attempt made by the President to substitute material for American manpower; this is basically the crux of the issue of military assistance. The Senate has seen fit to say we can have neither the manpower nor the material for our allies. I do not see, thus far, any outpouring of public support for the minority position, as it turned out, in the Senate.

HENRY PAOLUCCI: I am a professor of Political Science at St. John's University, where I have given a lot of attention in the past ten years to the Doctrine of Limited War that Dr. Kissinger enunciated years ago while serving on the Harvard faculty. Limited war is a question that concerns this Republican President, although it was first fought out under Democratic Presidents, namely Kennedy and Johnson. But in his book *Nuclear Weapons and Foreign Policy,* published in 1957, Dr. Kissinger summed up his long criticism of the policy of the Eisenhower-Nixon-Dulles Doctrine of massive retaliation in terms of Limited War.

You may recall that the Eisenhower-Nixon-Dulles doctrine of the 1950's said that in the effort to contain Communism, the United States was willing to go the whole way, that it would match every aggressive move with a counter move strong enough to do unacceptable damage on each level. There was no top limit to it. If the enemy pushed and pushed and pushed, the Eisenhower-Nixon-Dulles policy said we would go to the very top: the enemy must never think that he could, by military means, win his point.

The whole notion of the criticism that came out of the Council on Foreign Relations was that that was a dreadful situation, an escalation system that had the sky as the limit. Could something be done about it? Out of this came the doctrine of limited war. Limited war was a way of resisting communism; limited war was a way of using blood and weapons to resist communism, which would not necessarily go to the top. So the question always was, if you do not go to the top, how do you prevent the enemy from winning? For a while, in the 60's, people argued that we could do it; we could prevent the enemy from winning, even though we were not going to go to the top.

Then suddenly we found that by limited war we could not prevent the enemy from winning. Then people began to ask what is a limited war, then? And a limited war is then defined just as Henry Kissinger defined it in 1961. By definition, a general war is a war that the United States, or another major power cannot afford to lose; a limited war is one that a major power can afford to lose.

If the American people cannot support the Presidency now it is because we have asked 50,000 men to die in a war which the American soldier was never told was a war that the policy planners had said we could afford to lose. I would like to know this: Has Dr. Kissinger abandoned the doctrine or is he now getting our President to fulfill the doctrine that the Vietnam War is a war he could afford to lose, and now he is going to prove it by losing it? Now this is what I think is breaking the morale of the people of this country. And I believe it is a doctrine that was best defined by three men: McGeorge Bundy, teacher of Henry Kissinger; Walt Rostow, colleague of Henry Kissinger; and Henry Kissinger himself. It was adequately defined in two books: the first, Kissinger's *The Necessity for Choice* (1961) and the second, his introduction to a volume by many scholars called *Problems of National Defense*, (1965) wherein he defined national security in a way that goes beyond anything ever before given to it, namely that we could guarantee our national security either by winning or by not winning. I think that is a doctrine that must break the morale of any people who cannot support a foreign policy. I would like the comments of others, but particularly Mr. Sonnenfeldt's, since he works for Henry Kissinger.

WILLIAM CASEY: That is a good reason for me to answer the question! I would like to point out that the Vietnam War had been lost *before* Henry Kissinger became National Security Advisor to the President. And I would also like to make the statement that in my view, Dr. Kissinger and the President have done a brilliant job of achieving, substantially achieving, the objectives for which President Johnson involved us in Vietnam and mis-handled the involvement. Despite the lack of support and the political problems at home, a masterful job has been done of staying in there, and I think substantially the objectives for which we went into Vietnam have been achieved. And I give Dr. Kissinger a large part of the credit for that achievement.

HELMUT SONNENFELDT: Just two comments: One, that the issue in the middle 50's facing American military planners and American strategic thinkers was that the American nuclear monopoly had been broken. Two: that the doctrine of massive retaliation, that is to say, a doctrine that we would attack the population of another nuclear power, was no longer a credible doctrine as far as either our own people were concerned or people that were subject to attack. Moreover, it was no longer tenable for a President of the United States to be confronted in every contingency with only one military choice, which was to attack the population of the other side and risk the destruction of the American population in return.

What American military planners and strategic thinkers, leaving names aside now, were groping towards, and attempting to grapple with, all through this period, when the American nuclear monopoly was broken, was ways of conducting military strategy and procuring military forces that would solve this dilemma and produce for us a credible military strategy. They were seeking a strategy our own people could have some confidence in, that the people who had to be deterred could be deterred by, and that Presidents sitting in the chair where the button has to be pushed could have some confidence in and face with at least some equanimity.

This has been the job of the military planners and strategic analysts in the nuclear era. It is to find rational alternatives, to produce policies that are plausible, credible and feasible.

Now, what you have said about the Vietnam War, I substantially agree with Bob Ginsburgh, who was more closely involved in that, and he may want to say something. But I think we ought to be clear about the notions of limited war that we have discussed, that was introduced into American doctrine beginning in the late 50's and early 60's.

ROBERT GINSBURGH: I certainly agree with you, Mr. Sonnenfeldt, that at the moment the Nixon-Kissinger team has substantially achieved the objectives for which we entered the war in Vietnam in the first place. I say substantially because the war still is not over and the tide can still be reversed. But having said that, Mr. Casey, I do not quite see how you can in the same breath say that the war was lost during the Johnson Administration.

A couple of historical footnotes, on definitions and whatnot: while I basically agree with Hal about the kind of search we were making in the 50's for a new kind of strategy, I do not believe that much of the discussion on massive retaliation pays sufficient attention to the full phrasing of it, which was massive retaliation at instances and places of our own choosing. And that does not mean that in any circumstance, and every circumstance, we would automatically go to a general all-out nuclear war taking out the enemy's population.

The other point I would make is that in Mr. Kissinger's first book, referred to earlier, that is *Nuclear Weapons and Foreign Policy,* the emphasis was not on limited conventional war but on a less than all-out nuclear war—the use of nuclear weapons without necessarily an automatic escalation to an all-out general war.

BLAHOSLAV HRUBÝ: I sometimes wonder whether we are not headed for another Munich in 1972. But I have full confidence in President Nixon that, when he will talk to Mao Tse-Tung or Chou En-Lai and then to Brezhnev and Kosygin, he will do a better job than Mr. Neville Chamberlin of Britain and Monsieur Edouard Daladier of France did in Munich when they capitulated to Hitler and Mussolini and betrayed Czechoslovakia. This question, of course, has been recently asked by many people, friends of the United States, in Communist countries. I wonder if one of you would like to make a comment on this issue.

The second question is what are we going to say to millions of peoples in Communist countries because the Communist world is in trouble. Mr. Smrkovsky, the number two man under Alexander Dubcek, said in a recent interview in an Italian Communist paper that more than 90 percent of the people in Czechoslovakia are against the Soviet Union. And there is opposition in Hungary, Poland, East Germany, etc., and even in the Soviet Union and Red China. This is a great challenge for the Voice of America and other radio stations. How are they going to explain what happened during the past few days in the United Nations?

And the third question concerns the political and spiritual climate in this country. Some Americans almost enjoy to say how bad the U.S.A. is. I remember an American churchman who made the following highly emotional appeal to the General Assembly of the World Council of Churches in Upsala, Sweden in 1968 during a discussion of a resolution concerning the Vietnam War:

"Please make the condemnation of the United States stronger so that, when I return home, I can tell my congregation that the whole world condemns us." Such an emotional appeal, it seems to me, does not represent a responsible Christian search for truth and for an intelligent and ethical solution of difficult international issues.

ABRAHAM HOLTZMAN: I am a political scientist at North Carolina State University. I want to take up the question that General Ginsburgh stimulated. I raised it at the dinner table, and I would like to pose it to you, General. You did say that one of the problems we faced is bringing Congress into a greater degree of congruence with the President, and, I gather, the foreign aid bill is a beautiful example of the case at point.

We face, it seems to me and to many members of Congress, a dilemma wherein Congress by the Constitution has the power to declare war and yet the President, by the magnificence of his establishment and through his initiative, has in effect captured the power to make war, which really in effect is the power, unofficially, to declare war.

Now, a number of Congressmen have suggested; (1) that the President has a degree of unlimited power in this area; (2) that this is dangerous to our system; (3) and that Congress should be brought back into decision-making in this area through a proposal that keeps the degree of flexibility for a President to respond to crises and emergencies but which, at the same time, within a limited period of time forces Congress to decide on whether it wants to commit the American people and the American society to a continuation in armed conflict.

I am talking about something New York's senior Senator, Jacob K. Javits, has proposed in the Senate. His war powers bill says that if Congress does not declare war, there are four major areas of Presidential armed intervention (in response to treaty obligations, or attacks upon American nationals overseas, or attacks upon American forces overseas, or attacks upon the United States) where the President would be bound, as soon as he committed United States troops, to offer an explanation to Congress and a justification. Congress would then be forced within 30 days to act one way or another. Once it had acted, the President would be bound by the Congressional decision. Now, this does involve a limitation on the President's power as Commander in Chief. And I think we all agree here that the power of Commander in Chief has vast implications for foreign affairs.

ROBERT GINSBURGH: I think you have done a very excellent job of defining in some detail the problem that I have just alluded to. Now that we have defined the problem, it is up to somebody else to find a solution. And I think the solution has got to be found within the Congress and between the Congress and the President. I do believe that Senator Javit's proposal is a constructive proposal. But I do not think that this represents the answer yet. I do not pretend to have a better answer. I think the proposal is worth a lot of discussion; maybe it will turn out to be the answer, but I do not think so. I do not think we have found the key yet. And I again suspect the real key is most probably *not* going to be through a formally established legal restriction on the President's powers, but rather some way of returning to a system of greater consultation, of the President seeking responsible advice, not only from the Senate, but from the whole Congress.

Americans traditionally like to have their problems neatly boxed in and solved. But I do not think we are going to find a satisfactory answer in terms of a specific legislative proposal, like the Javits proposal, although I think discussion on it will hopefully lead us to a kind of institutional arrangement which would be better than we have had in the recent past.

JOSEPH GRIMES: I would agree wholeheartedly with the general on that. A procedure under which the President has to report to the Congress within 30 days and the Congress had to act would really put the Congress in a very difficult position. You would essentially have the same situation as you had with the Gulf of Tonkin Resolution. The President can present an issue in such a way that the Congress really has no choice. The important point in the future on the foreign policy of the United States is to bring about a greater policy consensus in the leadership of the country which includes the Congress and the President.

The problem has been that they have been pulling apart. The Congress has felt they have not been consulted often enough; and that the only time they were consulted on Vietnam they were had. Now, whether that is true or not, that is the feeling they have. Some kind of proposal like the Javits proposal is not going to force the kind of consultation necessary to create a new consensus. On the contrary, it will institutionalize the problem.

COLEMAN McGINNIS, Assistant Professor of Political Science at the University of Tennessee at Nashville: I want to ask Dr. Franklin if he realizes what the implications of his statement are for this need for idealism. I think General Ginsburgh talked about the only way we can have the time and energy to work on our domestic problems is to conduct our foreign policy successfully. I want to turn that around.

I just wonder if the only way we can restore some of this idealism and regain some of this confidence in our ability to govern ourselves is not going to be necessary to solve some of these very critical domestic problems that we talked about this afternoon. We must demonstrate that we can solve some of these extremely serious problems of poverty and housing and transportation and our own domestic economy. Only when we do can we conduct a foreign policy based on genuine self-confidence and exemplary conduct. Until we do we cannot sell the world the evangelical notion that we have the answers. This will come when we answer some serious questions about our ability to govern ourselves.

WILLIAM CASEY: That is a very interesting statement. You have to have exemplary conduct both at home and abroad.

GORDON HOXIE: May I offer just one brief concluding historical footnote with regard to the Presidency and the war powers. We can recall one undeclared war with the French within a decade of the enactment of the Constitution. Some referred to this as "Mr. Adams' War" which earned credit for the frigates, the United States, the Constellation, and the Constitution. Then little more than a decade thereafter a declared war, even more derisively referred to as "Mr. Madison's War," was fought with the British, i.e. the War of 1812. Both of these wars were criticised bitterly by the Congress, the first by the Democrats and the second by the Federalists.

Then three decades thereafter came another armed conflict opposed by many in the Congress. This was the Mexican War, referred to by the Whigs, including Abraham Lincoln, as "Mr. Polk's War." Indeed, it was in that war that Mr. Lincoln introduced his only notable resolution of his single term in Congress, his so-called "spot-resolution" demanding to be shown the spot where American blood had been spilled on American soil by Mexican troops.

Less than four score years later we were back in Mexico, this time in an undeclared war, directed by President Wilson, a "punitive expedition," with General Pershing chasing after Pancho Villa.

In brief, we can recall several declared and undeclared wars prior to Korea and Vietnam in which the exercise of Presidential power has been criticised.

The most decisive exercise of the powers of the Commander in Chief was probably by Presidents Lincoln and Washington. It was Washington who turned to his Secretary of the Treasury, Hamilton, who was a Major General, and called out the armed forces of the United States to collect taxes and destroy illegal distilleries that the Treasury's own agents were unable to cope with.

And it was Abraham Lincoln who exercised the most sweeping powers of the Commander in Chief, even suspending, in some instances, the writ of *habeas corpus.*

What I am saying in the final analysis is that the solution to the relationships between the President and the Congress in foreign affairs, and most particularly in regard to the President's role as Commander in Chief, cannot be legislated. The solution rather is found in the Constitution itself, the leadership of the Commander in Chief, the constant searching, understanding role of the Congress, and the faith of a free people enlightened by their representatives, by their President, and by a *responsible* free press.

This then concludes this evening's round table. Our warm thanks to Mr. Casey, his erudite panel, and to all of you for your intelligent participation.

CHAPTER V

Organization and Implementation of Policy

GORDON HOXIE: *Introduction*

Good morning, ladies and gentlemen! I hope I can say "Good morning, friends" after what has been for me, and I hope for each of you, a most stimulating weekend.

One of my very best friends didn't greet me very cordially this morning, and I wondered really what was awry. I refer to the distinguished Chairman of the Securities and Exchange Commission. He was sitting over in the corner this morning, buried in the *New York Times*. . . . I don't think his expression was related to the stock market or the national headlines, but he didn't invite me to sit down. A little while later I saw a very lovely young lady, Miss Bernadette Casey, sit down with him. I got up my courage and went over and said to Miss Casey, "I see you rate much better than I do with your father this morning!" Whereupon, it all came out. You see, I had left a message at the front desk that all of my staff should be called at 7:00 this morning. But they had called the wrong Casey! Instead of calling Bernadette, who had been undisturbed until 8:30, they had pounded on her father's door at 7:00 a.m. They told Mr. Casey: "Dr. Hoxie says you are to get up immediately and get over here!" So. . . Bill, please forgive me for routing you out!

Yes, this has been a weekend full of challenge with the topic "The Presidency of the 1970's." We opened Friday evening with three keynoters. Two were former Presidential Press Secretaries who had just returned from the Hill where they had testified before Senator Birch Bayh's committee as to whether there should be only one Presidential term. (You will remember they both indicated there should be no such limitation). In their keynotes they traced, with particular emphasis on the decades of the 1950's and the 1960's, changes in the institution of the Presidency. Mr. Hagerty's primary focus was on Mr. Eisenhower, and he concluded that "historians now agree that his [Eisenhower's] eight years of office look better and better as you look back on them." Hagerty emphasized that Eisenhower "had mastered the art of compromise, of achieving the common good without the surrender of principle and integrity."

Mr. Reedy, in turn, described "the decade of the 60's . . . in which the institution of the Presidency was brought to its sharpest challenge." He concluded that "there were always strains inherent in the office; flaws which were inevitable as there are flaws in all human institutions. But strains and flaws began to appear in the early 60's which led us into a terribly troublesome era."

The third keynote, that by W. Clement Stone, emphasized the personality of the President as an instrument in achieving Presidential goals, including such organizational changes as would best combine to eliminate these "strains and flaws."

Following these three Friday evening keynotes, we had yesterday three memorable round tables beginning in the morning with the arresting topic depicted in four key words or phrases: Security, Diplomacy, Freedom of Information, and Scholarship.

Then, in our afternoon session, we had representatives of the several Cabinet departments focussing on domestic policy; last evening our topic was national security policy.

What we have attempted to project here are the major issues facing the American President in the 1970's, whoever he may be. Assuredly we have gained from this examination a three dimensional view, i.e. of the powers, responsibilities, and challenges. We noted both the interrelationships between domestic and foreign policy and the President's greater power in the latter. We concluded that the President must effectively exercise the full powers of his office in meeting these great challenges.

It is suggested by some that there must be a better working relationship, perhaps some further organizational relationship, between the Congress and the President. The students are so concerned about that particular topic and about that relationship that they have made that the topic for the National Student Symposium next Spring: i.e. Executive-Congressional Relationships.

It was finally suggested last evening that the greatest of our Presidents have been those who have exercised the fullest force of their office as Commander in Chief, those who have, by example, inspired a national sense of purpose and determination to achieve working goals. In times of especial challenge Washington and Lincoln exemplified that kind of purpose.

But qualities of leadership must be combined in a complex society with effective organization if these "flaws and strains" are to be eliminated. Thus, this morning, we take up the organization and the decision-making process. Having reviewed and projected domestic and foreign policy issues and goals, we ask by what organization, by what decision-making and decision-implementing process are these achieved?

Last year the final round table was chaired by Thomas W. Evans, member of the law firm that formerly included both the President and the Attorney General. Mr. Evans is a very real student of government, not just from the vantage point of private law, but also of public law. He is the President of the Robert A. Taft Institute of Government, which is concerned, as is our own organization, with the study of political processes and the building of a sense of unity out of our diversity. A student of politics in action, he served as general counsel for the 1968 Nixon campaign.

Tom Evans is concerned with the attitudes of students and teachers toward politics. Perhaps some of you saw the article by Myron Farber in the *New York Times* in the Fall of 1970 on student attitudes. Therein Farber related the story of a Columbia University freshman who had a picture of the late John Fitzgerald Kennedy pinned to the wall in his dormitory room. One day the picture fell off the wall; the young man didn't put it back up because when it fell it suddenly crossed his mind that he really had no idea what John Fitzgerald Kennedy stood for. Tom Evans believes with us that that is a great tragedy not just for that generation but for our generation or any generation. When we say "Putting the Picture Back on the Wall" we are speaking in terms of the meaning of our Republic and its leadership. My very good friend, Mr. Thomas W. Evans.

THOMAS W. EVANS: Gordon, thank you very much.

This morning we are going to focus especially on decision-making, and, more particularly, on the mechanics of decision-making. In the course of this, we shall point up the question of how material gets to the President. How can he best mobilize and utilize his staff? How can he most effectively call upon his Cabinet, indeed all of the Executive Departments, including the Executive Office of the President, to help create, define, promulgate, and implement national policy. There is, after all, one door to the President's office and a telephone on his desk. The question of access is one of the most heatedly debated questions in Government today and probably always has been.

In part, this is a matter of organization. A great many studies have been done over the last several decades as to how to reorganize the Presidency. The classic report in the 1930's was the Brownlow Report, and we have with us one of the top consultants to the Brownlow Commission, Professor Harvey Mansfield of Columbia University. Professor Mansfield has written widely on government, the mechanics of government, and decision-making. . . . His books on the Office of Price Administration, in which he served, and on the Office of the Comptroller General and the General Accounting Office are classics in the field. More recently he has written extensively on the relationships between the civilian and military components of government.

After the 1937 Brownlow (officially termed the President's Committee on Administrative Management) Commission, there were two Hoover Commissions 1947-49 and 1953-56. Subsequent to the second Hoover Commission there were the studies led successively by Nelson A. Rockefeller, Ben W. Heineman, and Franklin A. Lindsay. In brief, there have been very, very many studies on our Government before the President's Advisory Council on Executive Organization. This so-called Ash Council can be considered refreshing if only because it uses the word Council rather than Commission! But we hope also there are greater things to come from the Ash Council. Already their recommendations for the Domestic Council and the Office of Management and Budget have found fruition.

Also with us this morning is one of the top aides of the Ash Council, James Finch, who is now top aide to the Citizens Committee which seeks to implement the recommendations of the Ash Council. The remaining members of our panel are Helmut Sonnenfeldt, who is one of the top aides of the National Security Council, the foreign policy arm of the President's immediate staff, and Dwight A. Ink, Jr., who prior to coming to the White House was Assistant Secretary of Housing and Urban Development, was Chairman of the White House Task Force on Education, and presently is in charge of Manpower and Systems for the White House as Assistant Director, Office of Management and Budget. As such he is the top man to discuss the question with the President and his aides on the manner in which the Government can be and should be organized.

Now to put organization in perspective. Forty years ago, in 1931, Herbert Hoover had two White House assistants. As the depression deepened and he built up Government to combat it, by the time he left office in March 1933, he had doubled his staff to four assistants.

When Franklin Roosevelt came into office, he was confronted with those four assistants, i.e. three White House secretaries and one administrative assistant. With characteristic sophistication and guile he did not make the designation of administrative assistant; because he did not want to show any favoritism on his staff. The Roosevelt Administration is illustrative of the era of the generalist. At this time when we are considering many different titles and structures, consider the jobs that were held by some of the great aides under Franklin Roosevelt. Thomas G. Corcoran, who had come into the Reconstruction Finance Corporation in 1932 under Mr. Hoover, became a speech writer who also drafted significant legislation for Mr. Roosevelt. His primary job with the RFC is often forgotten since it was way down in the federal hierarchy. Raymond Moley, Professor of Public Law at Columbia, became the top speech writer, sort of the chairman of the board of the brain trust. His job? Assistant Secretary of State. Rexford Guy Tugwell, Professor of Economics at Columbia, became another member of the brain trust. His job? Assistant Secretary and then Under Secretary of Agriculture. His intimacy with a plow in the field was almost unknown, but they had to find a way to pay him and a place to put him. Another brain truster drawn from Columbia, Adolf A. Berle, like Corcoran, was initially assigned to the RFC and then to the State Department. So this is the way things were done at the beginning of the Roosevelt Administration. The actual number of White House staff was not at first appreciably enlarged.

Since then, as I have said, we have seen a proliferation of assistants and an abundance of commissions and councils. The major enlargement began with the Reorganization Act of 1939, which brought the Bureau of the Budget from the Treasury to the White House.

The question remains, how does the man at the top of the pole, how does the man, as Harry Truman so incisively put it, who sits where "the buck stops," how does he make a decision?

How does he get help? What kind of input is utilized to help him?

As a starting point, I'd like to turn to Jim Finch, Executive Director, Citizens Committee for Government Reorganization, and ask Jim to give us, if he will, the recommendations of the Ash Council which call for a sweeping reorganization of the Federal Establishment.

JAMES H. FINCH, JR.: Thank you. As I'm sure most of you know, the President appointed the Ash Council in April, 1969, giving it a broad mandate saying in essence, "Tell me how you would best organize the Executive Branch of Government to operate more efficiently and to help me manage this vast system more effectively." The Council was very fortunate in the element of Presidential support. The President told them again, in essence, "You look at it; you analyze it; tell me what ought to be done, and I'll worry about the politics of it." The Council was not restrained by whether or not what they suggested was politically feasible and doable or not. The President took that burden upon himself.

In April 1970 in this Symposium a panel discussed the Domestic Council and the Office of Management and Budget proposals which were then pending before Congress. Those recommendations were based on two of the Council's 13 memos to the Presidents. As you know, the Domestic Council has been placed in operation and the Bureau of the Budget has been reorganized as the Office of Management and Budget. Three other new offices were also created in 1970 as a part of the Executive Office of the President. These are the Council on International Economic Policy, Council on Environmental Quality, and the Office of Telecommunications Policy. These then were the fruits of Reorganization Plan I, Plan II, additional Ash Council memos, and the Environmental Quality Act of 1970. In addition to the Council on Environmental Quality, a new independent agency, the Environmental Protection Agency was created in 1970, with William D. Ruckelshaus as the Administrator.

In 1971 we had the further fruits of a 1970 enactment, i.e. the change from the Post Office Department to the United States Postal Service. This meant the elimination of a Cabinet Department and the creation in its place of an independent Government corporation.

The Ash Council did a final study of the Executive Office of the President, which they called their overview and their final word to the President. In this they recommended deletion and transfer of some of the 16 separate organizational entities and 4000 people who currently occupy seats in the Executive Office of the President.

I would like to emphasize this morning the Council's recommendations on Cabinet reorganization. In the course of these two years the Council did extensive study of the domestic Cabinet Departments. These departments, which you are familiar with, have had a dramatic change in their program responsibility over the past two decades. We found that twenty years ago these departments operated something like 150 domestic programs. Today, the number is in excess of 1400. (There were nine of these departments then; there were 12 until the elimination of the Post Office Department this year).

Twenty years ago they dealt with a budget of something less than $40 billion. Today we are looking at a budget in excess of $225 billion. The fields in which they work, the things they have to work with, the responsibilities they are statutorily obligated to carry out, are vastly different.

The Council grappled long hours with these problems. We interviewed some four hundred people in the field and in Washington, inside of agencies and out, governors, mayors of small towns, all kinds of people who need help from these categorical programs. We found many of the frustrations they experienced trying to sift their way through.

The Council came to the point to recommend to the President a *very major* restructuring of these Cabinet Departments. In doing so they sought to organize around what they considered the *major purposes* of government. One such purpose they envisioned was *community development.* They recommended creating a Department of Community Development, composed of the programs of several existing agencies. (These include the Department of Housing and Urban Development; the rural development programs now in the Department of Agriculture; and certain elements of the Department of Transportation including the Highway Administration and the Urban Mass Transit Program). They also envisioned picking up other bits and pieces, such as the Community Action Programs in the Office of Economic Opportunity. The thrust of all of this was to pull together into one broad department elements whose overall mission would be Community Development. There would then be included as many program elements as feasibly possible having to do with the overall goals of community development. This then would result in the Department of Community Development which would include urban and rural development assistance, housing, highways and urban mass transit systems, and federal high risk insurance programs.

The other three new departments which are recommended are those of Economic Affairs, Human Resources, and Natural Resources. They, too, would pick up programs now divided among the Cabinet Departments and the independent organizations. Economic Affairs would include food and commodities, domestic and international commerce, science and technology, labor relations and standards, national transportation systems, business development, and social and economic information.

Human Resources would include health services, income maintenance and security, education, manpower, and social and rehabilitation services. Natural resources would include land and recreation, water, marine, atmospheric and terrestrial resources and technology, and Indians and territories.

Under legislation, as sent to the Congress by the President on March 25th of this year, the old departments of Interior, Agriculture, Commerce, Labor, Health, Education, and Welfare, Housing and Urban Development, and Transportation, together with a number of the supporting independent agencies would be eliminated.

It was *not* preconceptions but rather the *experiences* as we worked our way through the study that led to these proposals for overall Cabinet reorganization and consolidations. For example, we ran into a situation where the Transportation people were okaying a new road system through a community where the Health people were funding a project creating a new area-wide hospital. But the HEW assisted hospital would be 6 miles from the new Transportation assisted road! And there would be no easy access for the people! These kinds of illustrations you could pick up in every program area.

We also found many duplications. If the President of the United States were to wake up tomorrow morning and buzz John

Ehrlichman and say "I had a thought! What we're going to emphasize in the domestic area for the rest of this year is the Federal Government's domestic water and sewer grants. John, now I want to know how we do it, who's in charge, and how we go about putting the emphasis on this important area of water and sewer grants." John, in all likelihood would call our friend who is here on this round table, Dwight Ink, and say, "Dwight, who's in charge of waters and sewers?" And Mr. Ink would be forced to go back to Mr. Ehrlichman and say, "Well, John, we've got to get the Secretary of Interior here; we've got to get Secretary Romney from HUD here; we've got to get the Secretary of Commerce and also Mr. Podesta here because the Economic Development Administration has some significant programs in the area. We might need the Director of the Office of Economic Opportunity because they have some planning money that can be used in some instances. We've got to get the Secretary of Agriculture here because they have rural water and sewer programs!" This example is not as far-fetched as it might seem. Mr. Ink can relate by actual experiences what would actually happen if you got together such a task force. First there would have to be some defining of terms—like what is a water and sewer grant—because each of these departments has its own program founded in legislation, its own definition on how big a pipe is, how you hook them together, all, I might add, good programs meeting real needs but *impossible* to manage from an *overall* policy point of view.

I had the privilege of interviewing the mayor of a small town of about 12,000 population, which had experienced a 20% population increase over a three year period as the result of an industrial development nearby. As a result the waste treatment disposal plant was completely overtaxed, and there were no resources for enlargement of the facilities. The tax money from the industry hadn't come in yet.

The mayor called his Congressman, who put his administrative assistant on the problem. In a couple of weeks the mayor received a foot high stack of applications for federal water and sewer grants. He said to me "Hell, we don't have anyone among our 31 fulltime employees who could read those things, much less fill them out!" They engaged a consulting firm, paid them in excess of $20 thousand, and filled them all out in the hopes that one out of the five would come through. Sure enough, the municipality itself qualified for a HUD grant and the outlying area qualified for an agricultural grant, but there was a strip in between the two that didn't meet anyone's criteria where some 150 of the new families lived, and they were left out. It took some 18 months of negotiating and coordinating in the federal hierarchy to put a program together that would meet this everyday, real everyday, need for which the Federal Government had programs for this local community. The final decision, the final knocking of heads to put the two programs together, was made at the White House!

Now, what size pipe you use, or who has to give a little of their program to match another fellow's program, is not the kind of decision the President of the United States or his principal aides should have to be making. He only has the same 24 hours a day that you and I do. There are more important things that he and his staff should give their time to.

It is because of this overlap, the fragmentation of program responsibility, where we have two, three, even five Cabinet Departments involved in a simple program, that this reorganization becomes a necessity. In the present situation we have Department heads who, together with their bureaucracies, think they can do their piece of the job better than those guys in the other departments. It is a very human, very understandable phenomenon. But it cries out for reform. We have to reach for some kind of structure in the system, to eliminate as much as possible of the duplication, and to cut out the red tape so that these programs can be delivered to the people more effectively.

THOMAS EVANS: Jim, thank you very much for that overview on the President's Reorganization Program and its imperative importance. I'd like to call now on Professor Harvey Mansfield to get his views as to whether the Council recommendations would, really again in your opinion, enable us to better solve problems and better help the President in making his decisions.

HARVEY C. MANSFIELD: This is a big and amorphous subject. Instead of trying to present any general view of it, I would like to pick a couple of practical problems, or examples which seem to me to present problems, perhaps present a paradox, and, thereby, at least open up an area for argument or discussion. My general view is not one of opposition to the Ash Council's recommendations so much as a note of skepticism about what can be expected of them and what the results might be.

We have here a proposal for four super departments, so to speak: Human Resources, Natural Resources, Community Development and Economic Affairs, or Economic Development. That fairly well comprehends the kinds of domestic activities the Federal Government may be involved in.

There can be a good many reasons for organization or reorganization, some of them cynical, some of them personal to appointees, and that sort of thing. But a proposal of this sort, for broad super departments seems to have as its main rationale the improvement of coordination of activities that are divided or shared among a great many federal agencies, such as the example that Mr. Finch just used. That is to say, it is neutral in its apparent impact; it's not designed to give a thrust or emphasis or to deemphasize any particular activities the Federal Government is engaged in. It doesn't automatically tell you that there are things that are being done that don't need to be done, or ought not to be done, or things that are inadequately done and that ought to be given greater resources or greater emphasis. In general, coordination would be to enable the range of related activity to be pulled together in some kind of coherence, at some level short of the President, and to affect the President's decision-making process and responsibilities by getting a great deal attended to without calling it to his attention, or, if so, at any rate, to present him with a nearly complete proposal, just to check and make sure it's going to be all right.

Let me take two examples: Mr. Finch mentioned the Environmental Protection Agency. This has been established since the Ash Council came in. What does this do to these four Departments? The law says that no one can do anything that affects the environment without taking into account what it may do to the environment and letting the Environmental Protection Agency know about it and afford that agency the opportunity to be heard, to participate, and to give its contribution towards the solution.

The latest interest of the Environmental Protection people seems to be with activities of the Atomic Energy Commission, of all agencies, in the Aleutians, of all places. Here I refer to the proposal to the Federal Courts that they stop the Federal Government from setting off an explosion on an Aleutian Island until there has been at least further investigation into the possible consequences of such a business. This is a way of getting problems solved short of the President. The response to this proposal is a Congressional Act delaying the thing unless the President shall personally authorize proceeding. The Environmental Protection Agency presumably can cut across anything the Community Development Department would have in view—roads, facilities, structures, anything of that sort, power plants, any kind of physical resource developments, any kind of community resource development.

The Environmental Protection Agency is not set up on the same principle as the rest of the Ash Council proposals. It cuts across them. It introduces an element of consumer interest that may strike across the board most any of the other departmental activities and therefore require the President's attention as a practical matter in coming to any resolution of an issue that the Environmental Protection Agency may find itself involved with, which would otherwise be disposed of in any of these four super departments.

So it doesn't seem to me that you can reconcile an Environmental Protection Agency, having a free, roving commission to hold up any project it chooses, with the notion that if we only can get these four super departments, nearly everything can be settled in one or the other of them without having to take the President's time. That's one example.

Perhaps a more dramatic example, certainly one that was less anticipated than the Environmental Protection Agency, has just emerged since the middle of August. When the President announced his wage and price freeze for 90 days, he intimated that there would have to be something coming after that. Although the full shape of Phase 2 has yet to emerge, some pieces are in evidence. What is particularly in evidence? There is a Pay Board and a Wage Board. Where do they fit within a proposed super department of Economic Affairs?

Back in 1967, in the State of the Union message, out of the clear blue sky, President Johnson introduced the idea that the Labor and Commerce Departments should be rolled together into a single Department of Commerce and Labor. He did so without any previous preparation or recommendation for that. People looked startled and surprised, but it was in some sense in a smaller way a forerunner for a Department of Economic Affairs. As was related by Mr. Reedy in an earlier conference of this Center, that proposal was dropped because of the opposition of labor leaders.

Now we have the somewhat broader proposal and the Ash Council's supporting recommendations. But the first time the President really has to get something done in the field of economic affairs, namely some action in restraining price increases, what does he do? He doesn't come up with an emergency message saying we can't afford any more time talking about this Department of Economic Development; he doesn't even mention the Department of Economic Development; he comes in announcing that he is going to appoint a pay board and a wage board. Well, what are these bodies? They are bodies of businessmen and labor leaders and so on, depending largely on voluntary compliance for their effectiveness.

I looked at the TV news a couple of nights ago and had a glimpse of Ralph Nader denouncing the President and his proposals for devolving governmental power on private bodies, as the worst kind of delegation of power to private parties without any legal responsibility. This made some strange bedfellows of Ralph Nader and some other critics of the activities there, but the point is that the President, confronted with the need to get something done, has got to take account of where the heavy battalions are.

A reorganization that is bland and neutral with respect to the power of the respective bodies is unrealistic in dealing with the policies in which the battalions of political powers are evident and there. The Environmental Protection Act, which organized the consumer power, will be untidy across the rest of Government. The necessity of doing something about wages means bringing in George Meany, who stipulates not only that he be on this commission but once on it, that no one else can review what that board says or does. That would play havoc with a super department of Economic Affairs, if there were one.

These are largely hypotheses. They are not meant to oppose the whole thing. They are only meant to indicate the variety of considerations that must go into the organization and reorganization of governmental agencies and their relationships to the President. It is not, as it seems to me, susceptible of such an orderly disposition as a four-way set of departments which would comprise everything and relieve the President of the need of taking account of changing priorities, coalitions of power and influence, changing emphases and deemphases, and shifting in groups of society that are affected by the Government's measures.

THOMAS EVANS: Thank you, Harvey. I know Dwight Ink and Jim Finch are itching to reply. The gauntlet is down. However, before giving Jim and Dwight a chance to demonstrate that there is a wedding of concept and practicality in the Ash Council proposal and in the attempted reorganization of our decision-making, I'd like to get, if I may, the foreign policy aspects of decision-making into the discussion.

The National Security Council, when it was first established, was called by Harry Truman "Forrestal's Revenge." Truman made it a point of not using it, until the Korean War led him to become a very faithful, true believer in the mechanism of the National Security Council. Dwight Eisenhower, with his great concept of staff, did rely upon it, as have Presidents since then. And the question arises today in the popular press, who is really our chief foreign affairs officer? Is it William Rogers, who has the traditional role, or is it Henry Kissinger, who is the President's personal advisor and who heads the growing and impressive staff of the National Security Council? Can the two work well together, and do they jointly help the President to make his decisions? Hal?

HELMUT SONNENFELDT: Jim Finch has told us this morning about the President waking up and thinking about water and sewers, then calling John Ehrlichman and all the subsequent activities that gave rise to. Let me say in response that when the President wakes up and decides he'd like to take a trip to Peking, he only has to make one phone call, and there it is, all worked out and organized!

The problem of the relationship between the Presidency and the other agencies of Government in the national security field, i.e. the foreign affairs field, is not new. It has been with us at any rate since the Wilson Administration.

There is a sort of natural tension in Governmental relationships. I can only talk about the foreign affairs field now, but I suspect in some degree it happens in the domestic affairs field as well. There is sort of a natural tension between a President on the one hand, coming into office with particular ideas about the direction of the country, and certain commitments made to particular policies in his election campaign, and, on the other hand, the continuing agencies in the Government whose members sometimes tend to see these periodic arrivals in the White House as some intruders into their own guardianship of the national interest. They are the ones who continue year after year, after year. They are the ones who have to pick up after a President has come and gone. They are in effect the custodians of the continuity of American foreign policy, the custodians of the definition of the national interest in international affairs. This does set up a certain amount of tension between the occupant in the White House and the established agency or agencies.

In this Administration the effort was made to devise procedures that, at least, to some degree would bridge this different perspective, different approach, by the kind of system that we briefly touched on last night and that we discussed at some length last year. In this system of this President, this Administration, you get not only participation in the sense that people sit around the table or write memos to each other about decisions. You also get it in the sense that the views and the particular perspectives that the interested parts of the Federal bureaucracy bring to a problem, are fully heard, vented, and presented to the President.

Now, this argument has frequently been made: shouldn't the State Department, as the senior agency in the Government concerned with foreign affairs, be the agency that handles the coordination of all of this and presents it to the President? I used to think that that probably was the best way to do it, when I was in the State Department!

It's become reasonably clear to me that the Presidential perspective will always be in someways different from the perspective of the agencies. The President cannot make a foreign policy decision, a national security decision, without factoring into that decision its domestic implications, its implications for his own political fortunes, not only this year, or in future elections, but his fortunes in forging the kind of political consensus which has to be built around a decision.

There is no way in which Presidential prestige and influence in the Congress and in the country at large can be transferred to a subordinate agency of Government. The major departments of Government obviously have their influence, obviously can do a great deal in the Congress and in the country. Ultimately, in our system, however, it is only the President and the Presidency that on the close decisions, on the controversial decisions, on decisions where priorities have to be determined, can effectively act. Likewise, where some significant interest group may find itself disgruntled or disappointed by a decision, it is only the Presidency at that point which can present the issue and which has the prestige and the clout to put it over.

As we know, of course, even the Presidency in recent years hasn't been able to accomplish that. Nevertheless, there is no way of substituting the Presidential influence, the overarching Presidential appeal to the country, which cannot be obtained, which cannot be projected, by an individual Cabinet officer. Now that does mean that the President, in order to do these things, does have to have the staff assistance that is required to treat the issue from his peculiar perspective. That has given rise to the Presidential assistants in the security field. This began in a sense with Wilson and Colonel Edward M. House. It continued with Roosevelt where some of them were in the White House, but he tended to use some of them that were in the Department of State as well [Adolf Berle and Sumner Welles]. Even in the Eisenhower Administration, despite the overpowering personality and influence of John Foster Dulles, there were nevertheless over the eight year period in the White House a series of close advisors to the President in the national security field. Then in the Kennedy and Johnson Administrations there was McGeorge Bundy followed by Walt Rostow.

Now, is it only one or is it two or many advisors on national security affairs that the President calls upon? What is involved here is that the National Security Advisor to the President provides, first of all, the Presidential perspective on a problem. Here I refer to both the immediate perspective and the ultimate perspective, the President has to bring to it if he is to be an effective President. Now that, however, does not relieve the President of the necessity of bringing to his decision-making, the perspective of the senior official concerned with the impact on, the effects on, our relations with the outside world, and that is where the function of the Secretary of State comes in. It does not relieve him of the need to have a professional and expert judgement of the impact, the implications, of a given decision on our physical security, which is where the Secretary of Defense and the Chairman of the Joint Chiefs of Staff come in.

It is quite true that decisions may in the end be made only in a very small group, in some occasions only involving the Presidential Assistant. However, it is not the case that in the situation leading up to that final moment of decision that all these other aspects or elements and personalities are excluded. So the short answer to your question is "Yes, on occasion the President does pick up only one telephone." The long answer is "No, the President does not pick up only one telephone."

THOMAS EVANS: Well, that's the short and long of it. It's also I think as fine a short statement as we can get on this interesting and challenging conflict. There were a couple of elements you will notice introduced in the course of Hal's statement. One that was touched on briefly was this question of politics. We can't always study this question *in vacuo;* it's not always a question even of which functions most efficiently or economically. It may not, for example, always be the question of the best location for a given military base but rather in whose district would that base be located. And what's he doing lately? And whose side is he on?·

Also, Hal touched on the question of personalities. Some members of the Cabinet are perfectly happy and pleased to have their input go in through a staff assistant. They realize, or believe, that this may be the best way to do it. Others resign. So the question of personalities, as Mr. W. Clement Stone suggested in his keynote remarks, should also be considered in reviewing what might be the best way in enabling the President to make his decisions.

Before our break this morning, we would like to hear the observations of Dwight Ink, the man in the White House at the highest level charged with the responsibility of making our Government and Presidential decision-making in particular more efficient.

We have now had the recommendations of the Citizens Committee for Government Reorganization to reform the mechanism of this decision-making. We have had the views of a distinguished academician, Harvey C. Mansfield, who played a significant role in an earlier reorganization effort, that of the Brownlow Commission of 1937, raising questions about some of these recommendations. We have had the views of a senior staff member at the White House regarding the national security aspects of decision making. Now let us turn to Dwight Ink, primarily to respond to Harvey Mansfield's observations.

DWIGHT A. INK, JR.: First, Harvey, let me speak to your examples regarding Presidential involvement in decision-making. You refer to the Amchitka nuclear explosion. That is something that would go to the President no matter how our Government is organized. As a matter of fact, this is an item that went to the White House *before* the Environmental Protection Agency was ever recommended. It went to the White House *before* the Nixon Administration ever took office. These kinds of issues, can, do, and I think should, come to the White House. Where there is public concern, and there certainly is in regard to that particular item, regardless of the merits, of the pros and cons, it should go to the President. Indeed, any organization that inhibits that kind of thing from coming to the attention of the President, is one that should be looked at rather carefully. We had some of this in the early 50's, and I think it was undesirable.

In respect to the price-wage problem, Harvey, I would certainly agree that the President did not make any mention of the Department of Economic Affairs as the vehicle of carrying that out. I think it would have been rather ridiculous for him to have done so, since there wasn't the slightest prospect of that Department coming into being in time to have it make a practical effect on the then pressing price-wage issue. Economic Affairs was one of the four departments that have been proposed. Since each of these is very sweeping in its scope, and thereby by its very nature quite controversial, I think it was clearly impossible for the proposed Department of Economic Affairs to be looked upon as a vehicle for any part of the President's wage-price package.

It seems to me that there are several things that might be emphasized with respect to Presidential decision-making. Some of these have been somewhat touched upon today and also in our conference here last year. First, in order to provide an effective way in which a President can make decisions, those decisions which need to be made, and can only be made in many instances by the President, it is important to screen out those kinds of decisions which can be made elsewhere, which can be made at a lower level. It is important, of course, in the screening process, to screen the wheat from the chaff, and it is a matter of judgement, in individual instances, of course, as to what is so important, so significant, that it requires Presidential attention, and what is not.

But we have a system in the domestic area, and at one time we had one in the national security area, which works in reverse, which tends to force up to the Presidential level those sorts of things that ought *not* to be cluttering the President's time. It is those things in the domestic area which now press upon us for organizational reform. Those are the things which could more effectively, in many instances, be done by people at a lower level, by people who have more time, more information, more knowledge with respect to the particular subject matter.

Jim Finch mentioned the sharing of functions, which is one of those mechanisms which tends to force issues up. At the 7:30 meeting in the White House that Bob Podesta mentioned yesterday, we see this time and again. Although the 7:30 meeting is not the kind of vehicle at which those kinds of decisions are made, they emerge very briefly, and at the meeting someone is given the job of working on the issue raised and coming up with a decision. But when water and sewer problems in Des Moines, Iowa or Oakland, California reach that level, you know there is something wrong with our machinery. The fact nevertheless remains that if no agency head, or no Department head, has that program in its entirety, does not have the legal authority to make that kind of decision because it's shared with other agencies, then it is going to come up to the White House, and in a few instances, up to the President.

In order to meet this problem, because reorganization is very difficult to accomplish, very controversial, very difficult to get Congress to move in some of these areas, we resort to organizational crutches of one type or another. One of our favorite crutches is that of the interagency committee. We resort quite often to the interagency committee. As a matter of fact, we had about a year ago, 850 of these interagency committees that we resorted to. There's almost no mechanism as ineffective, as sterile of output and result, as the interagency committee. It is popular, not because it works, but because people have not been able to figure anything else out. It is extremely cumbersome for planning and policy, although occasionally I think it has provided a useful role of that type. I think it is generally disastrous with respect to operational activities.

I might say that over the past year we have cut out about 100 of those 850, and so far I have not found anyone around Washington who has reported any loss as the result of the 100 interagency committees disappearing. I am inclined to believed that if we could cut out four or five hundred more we still would not have anyone reporting any sense of loss. So, I think it is important to try to group functions, like functions, related functions, in one agency, to streamline the operations and to improve the accountability and to minimize the extent to which things are pushed up to the White House and the President for decision.

Clearly though, and I take this to be the implication of Harvey's remarks, you cannot do that in its entirety. There is no way in which you can organize the Government so that there are no related activities in different organizational units, short of the point of putting everything into one department. That is where it leaves you; so what you try to do is to come up with groupings that minimize the extent to which things cut across governmental and agency lines. That is what the President is seeking to do in his Cabinet reorganization program.

One of the things both the Ash Council and those of us engaged day by day in those concerns in Government agreed should not be lumped together is the regulatory activities. Harvey, this is the reason we concluded that the Environmental Protection Agency, which is essentially an agency to control environmental problems, should be left outside of departmental reorganization. It is rather those activities that are developed primarily, or engaged in primarily for the enhancement of the environment, which represent most of the environmental effort in the Federal Government, which are now scattered around Commerce, Interior, Agriculture and so on, that are brought together under the proposed Department of Natural Resources.

A second point I would like to emphasize, by using Jim Finch's example, is that the kind of water and sewer problem which sometimes comes up to the White House level, ought not to come into Washington, at all in most instances, to saying nothing of the absurdity of coming to the President himself. Indeed, in many instances such matters should not come into the Federal Government in the first place. There really is no reason why we should have to decide in Washington where Des Moines, Iowa ought to put a water tank. Indeed, I do not really think it is necessary for the Kansas City Regional Office to decide where the Des Moines, Iowa water tank ought to go! It may well be necessary for the Federal Government to exert leverage, perhaps very strong leverage, to try to insure that the water and sewer program that a city lays down and the water and sewer programs that are assisted by the Federal Government in the suburban areas are compatible, so that they fit into an overall system.

By contrast, however, to our water and sewer example, there are those kinds of decisions that go into seeing that certain national goals are met, such as in the civil rights area or in pollution control. These latter types of things probably cannot be handled very effectively, at least in their entirety, at the state and local area. There has to be Federal leverage and Federal decision-making in order to make those national goals come true.

But we have really not done much to develop the capacity of decision-making below the White House level. We have not done much to build it up at the departmental level though we have done some. We have not done much to develop the decision-making capacity out in the field of the Federal agencies, certainly not until the last year or two. Neither have we done much at the state and local level. And as a matter of fact, we have done a great deal to undermine the capacities of those state and local elements. We have particularly done a great deal, unintentionally I think, in the way of undermining the capacity of state and local governments.

We of the Federal Government have undercut the leadership of those state and local communities, in part, and in some cases with good reason, because we did not have confidence in their leadership. We have also robbed them of their capacity to do things by laying so many requirements on state and local governments. We have found these requirements so myriad that we could not count them! So, I developed a computer system to see if we could computerize the requirements which we had laid on state and local governments; that became a pretty big project in itself. We ended up by programming, by putting into the computer, only some of these requirements and restrictions that are laid on state and local governments!

The final point I would like to make is that the decision-making process has become extremely complex in modern day government because of the complexities of modern-day society. In the international area if one looks at the decision-making process of NATO, you find that it is an extremely complex process. If you look at the decision-making process in dealing with the revitalization of the modern city, the inner city that is deteriorating so rapidly, you find it an extremely complicated process. This is, in part, because of the involvement of the Congress, the press and the public.

Now, I do want to emphasize that in terms of policy development, particularly in these domestic areas, such as the inner city, it is very desirable and very necessary to have this public involvement. What I think we have *not* thought through too well, yet, however, is *how* that kind of involvement and *how much* of that involvement one can afford in the *operational* area. There must be a public involvement *balancing* with operational decision-making, by which there will emerge a workable decision-making process *and* a viable operational capacity. This is a balancing which is very difficult, and one on which I think a great deal of public attention should be focussed during the 70's, because I really do not believe we know how to strike that balance today.

THOMAS EVANS: Dwight, thank you very much. We have in this audience a very distinguished group of political scientists, commission heads, military leaders, men who have run state-wide and national political campaigns as related to governors, senators, and Presidents. We also have university presidents participating in this very vital question of decision-making.

Now putting the substance of policy aside, if we can, let us address ourselves to these questions: How can the Government, and the President in particular, be best equipped through our systems, to make a decision and then how can we best, through these systems, carry it into effect? I am going to ask our host, the chief executive officer of our sponsoring organization, the Center for the Study of the Presidency, if he will first respond to this question. He needs no introduction, but I would remind you that as a university head, as an Air Force general, and as a consultant to the U.S. Departments of State and Defense, he has himself somewhat uniquely participated in this decision-making and decision-implementing process.

GORDON HOXIE: Thank you Tom, you yourself so ably chaired that portion of our Symposium back in April 1970 when we took up a number of those issues, and Dwight Ink contributed immeasurably on that occasion, as he has here today by his cogent, succinct observations. When we met then the Ash Council recommendations for the redesignation and reorganization of the Bureau of the Budget as the Office of Management and Budget and for the establishment of the Domestic Council had just been made and were just being considered for possible adoption. Among those who made an eloquent plea here for the adoption, was Tommy Corcoran, who in his inimitable manner indicated that he wanted to see the Domestic Council, a rough parallel to the National Security Council on the foreign policy side, established because he hoped it would revitalize, bring renewed dignity to, the Cabinet Departments. He traced the decline of that prestige, as more and more government beginning with the Kennedy Administration had been conducted by Special Assistants to the President, and in the White House rather than in the Executive Departments.

Another participant in our 1970 conference, Walter N. Thayer, who was a member of the Ash Council, made, by way of example of the frustrations at the Executive Departmental level, rather direct reference to one Cabinet officer who at this present Conference is represented by his Under Secretary. Walter Thayer described the frustration of that Cabinet officer in not being able to see the President as often as both he and the President would like. Instead he was being constantly referred to a Special Assistant to the President. I say advisedly both he and the President because assuredly it is not the desire of this President to be cut off from his Cabinet officers. But the combination of the complexities of pressing foreign and domestic issues and of a multiplying bureaucracy had created a situation demanding of reform.

It is my own prediction that little more of this reform will be accomplished in the remaining year of the first Nixon Administration. If this is a pessimistic, it is nonetheless, I believe, a realistic, conclusion. The pressure of events, the controversial nature

149

of reorganization, the eve of the national election will all combine to postpone these reforms. It is my further prediction, however, that if this President in November of next year is offered a renewal in the White House, and this is not a statement of advocacy but rather of an assessment of facts, he will give high priority to the carrying through of his reorganizational proposals, to the streamlining of Government, to the reduction of the bureaucracy, including that in the White House itself, and to the transferral to the state and local levels as fully as possible the decision making as well as the operational controls of programs.

It is my further prediction that this President, looking pragmatically at the matter of reorganization, will, short of Congressional authorization, make such consolidations as he can.

Having made this projection to which I would invite Dwight Ink's comments, I would also like to ask Dwight a question: How has the Domestic Council worked out? It has now been in operation something over a year. Has Tommy Corcoran's reason for supporting the adoption proved a valid one? Has it brought a more effective relationship between the Cabinet Departments? And has it brought, may we say, better communications between the Cabinet and the Chief Executive?

DWIGHT INK: So far as your projection is concerned, Gordon, I am inclined to agree. Now, with regard to your question, you may recall that last year I said I thought it would be a mistake to try to assess the Domestic Council in the first year or two. In saying this let me again trace very briefly the history of the National Security Council which had a very uncertain early history. Mr. Truman had somewhat reluctantly utilized it, as Tom Evans expressed it, in his last years in office. The events of the Korean War had forced that utilization.

After some further experience in the Eisenhower Administration, there developed a great deal of concern that it had become too heavy a filter against seminal ideas. It was charged that the critical issues really didn't reach the President, that the NSC screened out the diversity of opinion and opposing influences in those basic areas that really ought to come to the President.

In the early days of the Kennedy Administration, in sort of a protest against that sort of situation, the NSC was almost utterly abandoned. We had the disaster of the Bay of Pigs and then a coming back to the National Security Council mechanism. Through the efforts of McGeorge Bundy and Walt Rostow the NSC became much more effective. Today with Mr. Nixon and Mr. Kissinger, and with able staff such as Mr. Sonnenfeldt, it has reached a new level of effectiveness. I would conclude: (a.) it will never be perfect; and (b.) it will be used differently by each President.

The first year of the Domestic Policy operation has exhibited some of the same kind of trial and error as occurred in the early days of the National Security Council. I think less so because, in part, it had that experience to draw upon. My own judgement, and this has to be very subjective, of course, is that it has been a very useful thing in the first year.

I say I am subjective because I have been an advocate. But I believe I can look back with some objectivity on the four administrations, including this one, in which I have served. Let me say that it is easy to find instances where it has not worked in the way it was supposed to work. But, to use that favorite Al Smith colloquialism, "Let's take a look at the record!" This is the first time where you will find the effective application of the principles Walter Thayer was talking about with regard to policy formulation in the domestic area. The welfare reform area is an example, where it has been applied. I think there are some that feel there is more that could have been done. I think some of us feel that conceptually the work was very good. Perhaps some of the machinery, the mechanisms, the managerial elements, were not factored in quite as thoroughly as they should have been. So I would say I think it has been very promising, but it is still in the early stages of development.

HARVEY MANSFIELD: I am indebted to my wife during the recess for another example which I would like to direct to Dwight Ink for his comment. This is the establishment of the Cancer Research Office in the Executive Office of the President. That led me to wonder if the President's motto had become "from the Ash Council to the ash can." Is this a case of trial, or a case of error?

DWIGHT INK: I am glad no one asks loaded questions here! Harvey, I did not happen to be one of those who recommended that! Under the concept that we are talking about, the broad mission-oriented departments, there are and will be, I think always, instances in which a President, and instances in which a Congress, sometimes the two together, feel so strongly about a given element, or a given problem, or a program. They feel it has to be singled out for very special treatment, for very special attention and for very special organizational arrangement.

Cancer is one of those that the President feels is so important. The problem is so significant for the health of the nation that he felt it needed that kind of special attention. Now I am sure, Harvey, that not very many of us would disagree with you as regards the hazards of the principle which you have enunciated. If you have very many of these kinds of exceptions, the exceptions begin to become the rules and, Harvey, I think there is a very real danger of that kind of thing developing. Again, I would add, Harvey, that there was the matter of a timetable. The creation of a cancer agency could not, should not, have to await the creation of the four new departments, including the Department of Human Resources.

THOMAS EVANS: I see the hand of another student of political science, John A. Wells, senior partner of one of the nation's foremost law firms. Jack Wells has not only written about government, but he has also effectively engaged in it at the state, local and national levels, including the political campaigns.

JOHN WELLS: I dislike the format of being asked to state a question when what I am really going to do is state a view! I will try to state a view and then ask for comment, if that is all right with you, sir.

It seems to me that in the days since Herbert Hoover was in the White House and started out with two assistants and ended up with four we have had some changes in both numbers and principles. Today there are many hundreds in the Office of the President, and the President has all sorts of assistants right under his eyes. We have gone from a super corporate form to the conglomerate form in effect, although one cannot push the analogy too far.

Now, it seems to me that when you are talking about the organization of the White House and decision-making, there is another thing you ought to be talking about at the same time. Here I refer to *effective implementation of the decisions that are made.* I think it was Lyndon Johnson who said that the President proposes and the bureaucracy disposes. If they do not want to do something, they are not going to do it. Of course, that means that the President has to seek some method of *seeing* that they do it. And in our lifetime, in our working lifetime, I think all of us have seen an effort on the part of Presidents, beginning with Roosevelt, to reach out into the Departments and agencies which were originally very autonomous, and in effect, independent duchies.

When we are talking about the structure of the White House, it seems to me that there are two possible structures. There is the traditional one, as in Hoover's time, where he had a pyramid. The President was at the top, and the departments and agencies were in the next line. The Cabinet was *really* a meeting of the heads of the various departments. Whatever in the way of information and views which were to come up, came up through the offices of the various departmental Secretaries.

Well, that is not what happens any more. Today, it seems to me that the White House organization is a circle. At the center of the circle is the hub. The hub is the President and the Office of the President and all the people located in the White House. Now there is *very good* reason for this, and I am *not* one of those who favor going back to the old independent department and agency format. I think the old format is completely unrealistic today from a minute to minute crisis management point of view.

One thing that nobody has mentioned is the absolute necessity that there be some kind of political consistency expressed with respect to the country and with respect to the Hill. And there again we have seen power steadily sucked from the legislative branch over to the Executive. When it gets over to the Executive, power cannot be dispersed. It has to be centralized and rationalized and made internally consistent. My question is do you disagree with my analysis, and if so, I would be very glad to hear the reasons you do disagree.

THOMAS EVANS: Now that we've had a comment, is there a question from the panel? Let me just say this. I think this is really the kind of thing we were hoping for. Jack Wells is a very prominent lawyer. He has run successful campaigns for senators and governors here in New York State. This is the kind of input we have in this audience! Is there someone here who disagrees with his view, which seems to be at the very least contrary to the Ash Council, at least some of the Ash Council's recommendations, for placing greater responsibility and authority back at the Cabinet level?

HARVEY MANSFIELD: Mr. Wells has an interesting, provocative view. The reference to conglomerates is somewhat unique. I suppose the chairman of the Ash Council was an expert on conglomerates, if anyone in the country was! After all he was President of Litton Industries, which by the way, has not been doing so well! Your observations at the least coincide with the experience of 35 years. No matter what anyone has said about pushing things back down into the departments, the fact is that the Executive Office of the President has grown larger. It is true that from time to time pieces of it either because they become operational or get unwieldy are pushed further out.

Back in 1954 under President Eisenhower (and then Vice-President Nixon) there was the Kestnbaum Commission on Intergovernmental Relations. (This was named for its chairman, the then President of Hart, Schaffner and Marx). This led to an Advisory Commission on Intergovernmental Relations, which for a time was relatively close, though by the time of the Johnson Administration it was sitting out at 1800 G. Street. At any rate, if this means anything it's back now at 726 Jackson Place, at least within view of the White House. Where once it was a part of the Executive Office of the President, it is now technically an independent agency. That sort of transformation still goes on.

GORDON HOXIE: I agree with Mr. Wells that the centrifugal forces, driving things away from the center, the Presidency, are not as great as the centripetal, i.e., those attracting agencies and individuals around the Presidential Office. This President has already reduced the civilian employees in the Executive Branch by more than 100,000 since he entered office, when they numbered 2,960,823. He will probably meet his goal of an additional 100,000 reduction before January 1973. [Editor's note: civilian employment as of September 1972 was down to 2,767,872.] What he has not thus far done is to reduce the White

House bureaucracy which at the end of 1968 numbered 1,992 and at the end of 1970 had indeed, risen slightly to 2,071, of which approximately 600 are top aides and their staff.

THOMAS EVANS: Dr. Hoxie, I am inclined to agree with your prediction. Again, if I may make a prediction, it would be that there will be no reduction in this bureaucracy in the remaining year of the President's first term. [Editor's note: the number in the Executive Office of the President did increase in this 1971-72 period]. My further prediction, however, is that in a second term, if re-elected, Mr. Nixon will in keeping with the principle of the Ash Council seek both to reduce the White House staff and send many of its functions back to the Executive Departments. Mr. Wells referred to the Hoover Administration with four administrative assistants. Systematically such a relatively simple organization would appear to have provided a powerful engine for immediate action by the President, and yet we did see what happened.

In combatting the depression and in implementing the New Deal social legislation, by 1939, before World War II, the large modern Executive Office of the President had begun to evolve. Did this make the President more effective in exerting the Presidential will?

In at least two instances, I can think of two very miniscule things which indicate the effectiveness of carrying out that will. One was Richard Nixon's attempt, eventually successful, to remove those old grey buildings from the mall that had been there since World War I. The President said one day: "I'll have those out. They're very unattractive. They serve no purpose." What did it take? It took nearly two years to have them removed. As John Price put it, this is an example of "raw Presidential power." John F. Kennedy, when he was asked why he was spending so much time personally on the renovation of the buildings on Lafayette Square, just across from the White House, replied "Because it may be the only thing that I will be able to get done while I am down here, and I want to carry it through."

COLEMAN McGINNIS: As a political scientist, I am troubled by the concept that has been raised by several people. Perhaps Professor Mansfield would comment on this notion that we can separate the question of organization from the question of policy. It seems to me that arguments over organization

155

really center on the notion that, if we are dissatisfied with the policy output, we can resolve that by coming up with a new organization.

We are not operating in a vacuum. I am not certain that we can resolve the issue that there is a single best way to organize the Presidency. At any rate we have not done so yet. There seems to be a great deal of debate as to which is the best way to organize it. We are operating in a situation where we believe that the best organization, the most rational organization, the most efficient organization, is the one that is going to result in the policy output that we want.

It seems to me that we are being extremely unrealistic in our talk about organization when we try to divorce organization from policy. We are in a situation where, particularly in the reorganization of the Cabinet Departments, as Mr. Ink indicated, if you carry this concept of relationships far enough, what you will end up with is one consolidated department. One of the reasons the Congress isn't going along with this is because this would require tremendous reorganization of the Congressional Committee System in establishing effective Executive-Congressional relationships. The groups and individuals who have access under the current system do not want to lose that access under a new system.

It really seems to me to be typical of the kind of thing that has come out of the academic community. Political scientists have been extremely guilty of this for many years. We talk about what is the most rational way of organizing something without taking into consideration what is going to be the policy output from that. I, too, have made a statement and would appreciate some argument!

HARVEY MANSFIELD: I have just put something in print. I will send you a reprint of the God's truth on this subject! I think there is a distinction to be drawn. The minute you start talking about reorganization *in any given sector,* then immediately the policy consequences of any reorganization *in that sector,* loom large. For example, you cannot talk about what to do in cancer research, environmental pollution, that sort of thing, without getting into just that.

On the other hand, if you are thinking about *across the board reorganizational* changes, then I think it is a prior condition for success that you adopt a stance of neutrality towards the existing policy. In the first Hoover Commission, i.e. the bi-partisan Commission on Organization of the Executive Branch of the Government, Mr. Hoover himself had a combination of motives. He wanted to see things rationally organized, but he also wanted to retrench a lot in the government activities and thought that there were billions that could be saved by cutting down on expenditures. This Hoover Commission, created by the Congress in the summer of 1947, in 1948 came to something of a crisis. Some of the task forces had come in with recommendations that looked to policy changes that would comprise drastic retrenchments. To have adopted any of those task force recommendations under those circumstances, would have amounted to the Commission's endorsement of Dewey for President against Truman for President!

While it was a balanced Commission with four Congressional, four Executive and four private members, equally divided between Democrats and Republicans, all carefully balanced, this might have torn the Commission apart. So the Commission then had to adopt from the force of circumstances, with the approaching 1948 Presidential election, an attitude of neutrality. I might add that they did submit 270 specific recommendations, of which 70%, with President Truman's support, were adopted. Considerable overlapping and waste were eliminated. With even a wider mandate the Second Hoover Commission, that of 1953-56, came in with 375 recommendations. Many of these, in turn, with President Eisenhower's support were adopted.

What I am saying is that to be successful in broad areas of reorganization, these Commissions and the Congress and President must arise above politics to secure success. They must not be geared to carry out a particular program. Whatever the Government is doing, at whatever level, must be acceptable for a successful approach to broad reorganization. What we are trying to get is a rational rearrangement of the full structure of organization. And I think that the Ash Council, in talking about these four departments, is implicitly operating on this sound premise. They are not saying we ought to double welfare outlays, and the way to do that is through reorganization. They are taking the existing level and projecting an organization flexible enough for change. That means quite wisely a degree of separation between questions of organization and policy output.

157

THOMAS EVANS: Jim, do you feel the Council either elevated organization above, or ignored policy?

JAMES FINCH: No, the Council did not. The Council operated within the mandate the President gave it, and that was organizational. He said take the programs that exist, the enabling legislation that exists, tell me how best to structure it and manage it.

Let me say one additional thing. You have been referring in the last couple of days to "super departments." Inevitably when you get into a discussion of reorganization on the Cabinet level, and you talk about consolidation and reducing the number of Departments, people always say "God, you're creating a bunch of HEW's, when everyone knows HEW is unmanageable!"

You remember the discussion yesterday when it was said people often get into a position of power in one of these large organizations and start pulling levers and pushing brakes, and it seems the levers are not connected. In the course of our research we found that to be true. They are in fact, in some instances, not connected, and it's not an accident or wear and tear from normal operations that wore out the linkages.

In the HEW case, if you go back and read the legislative history of the debates in Congress, in the early 50's, that resulted in the legislation for the creation of HEW, you will find again and again a Congressman on the floor, in a Committee hearing, saying "We are not creating a czar of health, education, and welfare. These are important programs for the individual people, and the Congress must keep a hold upon the operations of each program." Consequently, when Mrs. [Oveta Culp] Hobby took the reins of HEW in 1953, it is not too much of an exaggeration to say her managerial power at that time consisted of assigning office space and passing out paper clips.

To this day the U.S. Commissioner of Education reports to the committees on the Hill that deal with educational legislation. The same is true in the welfare area. The same is true in the health area. With all due respect to the outstanding incumbent, Elliot L. Richardson the Secretary of HEW has little to do with creating the program or with the control of the program operations.

The same is true, as Mr. Ink said, in the field structure. There are 39 program people in each office of the 10 regional offices of HEW. They do not report to the Regional Director of HEW in

Dallas, or New York, or wherever he may be, who, in turn, reports to the Secretary. They report instead to their counterpart in Washington. Under the present policy formulating mechanism, you have little managerial ability fully utilized at the top of some of these departments in really running, managing, or implementing policy that has been made.

The reorganization proposal that the President sent to the Congress on March 25th is significantly more than just moving boxes and shuffling programs. Contained in that legislation is a significant strengthening of the Secretaries of these new departments. This would give them the authority, in many instances and in many programs for the first time, to actually run the programs. It is tough from the White House perspective, to manage a program, using the water-sewer illustration used this morning, if there are no persons accountable.

Roy Ash said from time to time in the meetings of the Council that *when many people are responsible, no one is responsible.* There needs to be a person, a general missionary of Federal Government programs that the President can hold accountable for the operation of those programs. If he has four Cabinet officers who are accountable, in varying degrees, for operations in a specific program area, it is extremely difficult to change anything. That is where we are now and why the President's proposal needs support.

HARVEY MANSFIELD: Mr. Wells' point is well taken, that the old pyramid concept really does not work. You have a whole series of agencies with powers and responsibilities, but for any given program, in any given time, it is going to take a cluster to get something done. The President does, indeed, as Mr. Wells stated, need a staff working for him that will do that.

I am sorry Mr. Sonnenfeldt had to leave, because I would like to quarrel with his view on that. In talking about whether Dr. Kissinger, or Secretary Rogers of the State Department ought to be handling a particular matter, I thought he would be more persuasive if there was any evidence that Henry Kissinger was some sort of an expert on domestic repercussions. Henry Kissinger is not any Lou Harris or George Gallup or anyone like the Director of Communication, Mr. Herbert Klein, or the Press Secretary, Mr. Ronald Ziegler, or the Secretary of Transportation, Mr. John Volpe, or the Chairman of the Republican National Committee, Senator Robert Dole, who have their pulse on domestic Affairs!

What you can say for Henry Kissinger, aside from his obvious ability, is that he is working for the President. By contrast somebody working for the State Department is working for the State Department, as well as for the President, and regrettably those two are not necessarily coincident all of the time.

Mr. Wells is suggesting that the President needs some people that are working for him, who, as each hot subject comes along, assemble perhaps *ad hoc,* perhaps in some more or less durable committee form, a working group that will bring together whatever is the relevant cluster for that particular problem. I also agree with Mr. Wells it may not necessarily be the same cluster from one problem to the next.

THOMAS EVANS: I think the organizationalists tend to say that what they are trying to do is to predict the *right clusters,* if they can, so these can be utilized. By so doing they seek to insure that the President will not miss an important ingredient in the decision making when that crisis comes along. I see the hand of Dr. Henry Paolucci, St. John's University, Political Scientist.

HENRY PAOLUCCI: The comment that I would like to make, which is the basis of a question, is that historically we have had three great forces impinging on our President. These are: (1) the productive forces that produce the Commonwealth; (2) the protective forces without which the Commonwealth soon ceases to be yours; and (3) the directive forces. Traditionally you had to have the first two, the industrial-military complex, secure before you could have government directed by discussion, as Walter Bagehot used to say.

Now when you try to coordinate these three elements of the pyramid, at the top, there is one of the three, i.e. of the productive, protective and directive classes that tends to monopolize by its very nature any coordinating effort. Here I refer to the directive class. If we forget that each is a vested interest, production, protection, and direction, we make the mistake of thinking that we can have some kind of neutral composite force surrounding a President in a cluster.

Now what we have been witnessing around the President is

that the productive and protective spheres get to be filtered through a directive sphere, which is obviously better equipped to produce "options." This is especially the case with the National Security Council. In the NSC we have surrounded the President with people who *only apparently* do not have a vested interest and purpose, and who only *apparently* seem to be filtering, screening and coordinating things when in fact they bring in an absolutely *predetermined* conception of what our foreign policy should be. That's bad enough there. I dread the day when we will *also* have it in the domestic sphere.

Now I submit that an advisory class of academicians is a very fine luxury for a nation. Provided, however, that the national production is secure and adequately defended. As Walter Bagehot said: "First, forceful unity, then felt unity, and then government by discussion."

We forget that when our great liberal, Wilson, came in, he espoused this Bagehot concept. Mr. Nixon has Woodrow Wilson as his ideal. But he has inherited a system made up of people who put discussion first, who even debate such a question as to whether our nation should remain sovereign as it approaches its 200th birthday. These people surround the President with that kind of thinking.

Now, I think this climate poses a grave danger structurally. These people pose as being more flexible, more moveable. They crowd around the President saying "I'll filter what the productive class wants, what the mean manufacturers, the military, and the police want!" But in reality they have a vested interest in that hostile view of sovereignty it is possible today to cultivate at Harvard and MIT, and certain other seats of learning.

THOMAS EVANS: I am going to be interested in what the panel is going to say. I do recall that Plato wrestled with this one quite a few years ago. I have a suspicion there may not be a pat, handy answer to it.

DWIGHT INK: I'll take the first cut at it. I'll start out talking about how the system is *supposed* to work, recognizing, of course, that systems never completely work out the way they're supposed to. But one of the objectives, the purposes, of the Domestic Council idea was to, in part, do just the opposite of what you are concerned about. It was, in part, to provide some assurance that on a given domestic issue there would be no pervasive power elite, be it academicians or others.

One of the concerns about the way in which domestic policy has been developed over the years, and the concern has been increasing in recent years, is that some of the White House staff, some of them extremely able, bright, have had a tremendous influence. It is stated that the staff have an influence beyond that of the Cabinet members and their staff, who have responsibilities for these areas. This is said so far as influencing the President in key domestic decisions, with respect to development of new policies and submission of new legislation. Because of the rather haphazard way, and sometimes rather cozy way in which this has evolved, agencies and departments that had not the primary role perhaps but had nevertheless a very significant role, were on occasions not even involved at all. There was concern, for example, about the way the Model Cities program was developed. I think if you will go back through that history you will find that a department such as HEW, which has a very important role in Model Cities as it was proposed and passed, had a very minor role in the formulation of that proposal. Consequently, it was rather difficult to generate enthusiasm within that agency for a partnership role in Model Cities. It was very difficult to find dollar support in HEW for the Model Cities Program. You can find many, many other examples of this kind of thing.

All right, the Domestic Council consists of the Cabinet members chaired by the President. The Domestic Council is *not* White House staff. There are White House staff who service the Domestic Council and who affect the departments and agencies by providing staff support for the Council. If the Council works the way it's supposed to, it really brings back into focus the kind of role that the departments and agencies ought to have with respect to advising the President on key issues. I think that the concern has been, and continues to be, that it may *not* work the way it is supposed to. The concern is that as a practical matter, the staff may really constitute the Council, with the membership left in the background. I would submit this is an issue as to *how* it's carried out *rather* than the *design* of the organization.

HARVEY MANSFIELD: I am not from Harvard or MIT but Columbia, so I cannot claim to be part of the glory of this nation! Nonetheless, I would suggest that the three-way categories of production, protection, and direction are a rhetorical figment of Professor Paolucci's imagination. It does not correspond with any reality in practical political terms. What does he mean by the productive? Does he just mean manufacturers and the financiers, or George Meany and the labor unions, who, too, make some claim of being productive? If they are all supposed to be agreed on the same thing, they haven't been showing it lately! But what the directive element is, I'm sure I don't know. It doesn't correspond with any real political forces.

THOMAS EVANS: That was a question of categorization. I do think that the final barb of his question, which had to do with the proximity of anonymous aides, or aides who are not departmental heads, is really the thrust of it. That may be at the heart of our entire discussion.

GORDON HOXIE: Since the growth of the Federal Bureaucracy keeps coming up, let me just add an historic footnote regarding the increase of Federal civil servants. The great increase began in 1933 with the New Deal. The increase from the pre-World War I era through the Hoover Administration had only been from 370,000 to 583,000. But by 1939, before World War II, the number had increased to 920,000. The first major decrease has been with the Nixon Administration. Modest albeit, I do predict a major effort at reduction of the Federal bureaucracy in the 1970's.

THOMAS EVANS: Gordon, we always appreciate your historic notes! The chair now recognizes the question of Dr. A. J. Wann, chairman of the Department of Political Science of the University of Utah.

A. J. WANN: This is mainly aimed at Mr. Ink, Mr. Finch, and Harvey Mansfield. When the National Domestic Council was set up, I think one of the principal objectives was improved coordination, to help the President do what only he has the responsibility for doing, i.e. of coordinating all the activities of the Executive Branch.

Many of us who have studied the New Deal period to some degree, thought back almost immediately to the National Emergency Council which Roosevelt set up rather early in his Administration and which continued as a sort of shell-like thing clear down to the Reorganization Act of 1939.

It became quite clear that the National Emergency Council never worked effectively as a coordination agency. It did serve some other purposes. I think Roosevelt likened it to a New England Town Meeting, and said it was a "fine exercise in democracy," as I recall. It was good for Roosevelt to get the Department heads and the heads of the emergency agencies together for an exchange of views. But it never effectively worked as a coordinating agency. This was mainly because Roosevelt never delegated and backed up, tangibly, his authority to the Council Director, Frank Walker or his successor, Donald Richberg. People like Harold Ickes, Harry Hopkins, Frances Perkins, Henry Wallace, and Jesse Jones would not go through Walker or Richberg to get to the President. In Robert E. Sherwood's terms, Walker was excellent at spreading oil on troubled waters. But the Council did not really function in an effective coordinating way.

Now what is really happening with the new national Domestic Council in this regard? Presumably Mr. John Ehrlichman is the director in a role similar to Walker and Richberg, and President Nixon is the chairman, just as Roosevelt was of the National Emergency Council. You have also, it seems to me, waters that are fairly muddy in this field. Mr. Robert Finch is around, in the White House, dealing with all sorts of domestic things. You do not hear so much of him any more, but he is presumably still close to the President. Daniel Patrick Moynihan did help, I guess, by going back to Harvard. Getting one strong personality out of the scene, cleared the air a little bit and removed some of the hotness out of it, I suppose. But there is the omnipresent George P. Shultz with his fingers in practically everything in the Government on the domestic side. As he was a colleague of mine in the industrial relations field years back, I am not casting any aspersions on Dr. Schultz's abilities, which are great, but merely indicating what appears to be a somewhat cluttered field of a group of able people all working on domestic affairs in addition to Mr. Ehrlichman.

Now we have the Cost of Living Council headed by Mr. John B. Connally, Jr. and with Arnold Weber and Donald Rumsfeld holding important positions. Perhaps above all, many of us have difficulty in picturing Mr. Connally going through Mr. Ehrlichman to get to the President.

You get down to personalities on this don't you, Mr. Ink? Who is doing what? Is Mr. Ehrlichman really the President's man in this whole picture? Do the Cabinet officers go through him in terms of coordination? Hearkening back to the New Deal is this just again an exercise of a sort of Town Meeting of bringing people together for exchange of views without really effective coordination?

DWIGHT INK: I suppose there are occasions in which some Cabinet members feel that they are going through Mr. Ehrlichman, when they ought to be going directly to the President. First, I would like to emphasize that it was not the intent of the advocates of the Domestic Council to set up a mechanism whereby Cabinet members had to go through someone on the White House staff in order to get to the President. As a matter of fact, it was intended to have somewhat the opposite effect. It was intended to be a mechanism in which there were two, or three, or four Cabinet members who were involved in a given area. Then, even though there might be a lead department, all of the involved Cabinet members would have the opportunity to debate that issue in the presence of the President, *after* there had been a great deal of staff work laid and ground work laid on that particular issue. So it was *not* the intention, and I think it ought not to be the design of any kind of mechanism of that sort to force Cabinet members to go through a staff man in the White House on substantive matters, although it may be on informational matters.

Secondly, the Domestic Council is concerned with policy, *not* operations. It is concerned with operations as they are related to policy, but the Domestic Policy Council is not intended as an operational vehicle. It is concerned with reviewing the existing policy and hopefully concerned with formulating a better and improved policy or perhaps policy that is more attuned to current conditions. You have really different mechanisms concerned with the operations. The OMB is heavily involved in an operational sense. Although it does not issue directives to the departments, it provides the staff support. The 7:30 meetings that we mentioned several times are a mechanism for teamwork, working together in an operational sense. In those 7:30 meetings, there are about 20 of us including the aforementioned

George Shultz, John Ehrlichman, Bob Finch, and Don Rumsfeld. These are the people that constitute that group each morning. We try to tie together the operational matters that need to be dealt with at the White House level, generally over the next 24 hours.

EDWARD C. LYON: I have, I am happy to say, been associated with Dr. Hoxie at C. W. Post College. Emulating him, I am a servant in the field of education.

It seems to me that one of the problems which exists is related to pressure groups. After these groups have been granted audiences by Government, and decisions have been made, these individuals do not accept their responsibilities to let decisions produce results. Instead they continue to lever, to hammer and to barter. Thus we do not have an opportunity to see if government can produce.

I wish more citizens, like those of us here, would take the time to say to the very fine men in government: "We understand that government is an acceptance of the wishes of many people. We desire to give government officials time to get decisions rolling and produce results."

THOMAS EVANS: Thank you for those cogent observations regarding access of citizens' views. I see the hand of Dr. Joseph P. McMurray, President of the College of New Rochelle, who had such experience in the federal, state and city governments.

JOSEPH P. McMURRAY: It seems to me that as you reflect upon the recent administrations, i.e. the Truman, Eisenhower, Kennedy, and Johnson Administrations, you find in each case that if the President really wanted to do something, he seemed to believe he had to set up a new kind of organization. Here I am referring to important policy changes, not day to day policy. It has seemed, and I believe erroneously, that such organization concepts provide the only effective way to major program accomplishments.

Let me give an example: housing. Here they organized the Department of Housing and Urban Development. But in this present credit crunch and, indeed in the era of the 1960's the Federal Home Loan Bank Board and the Federal National Mortgage Association, Fanny May, have really done more in the field of housing than HUD (founded in 1965) in terms of maintaining the housing starts and allowing the housing industry to contribute its economic might to our economy.

This observation implies no particular criticism of Mr. George Romney, who did stimulate housing starts, or of his predecessor of the Johnson Administration, Robert C. Weaver, who relatively did not. But what I am saying is that more than the department is the leadership of the man. For example, Arthur Goldberg, as you know, played a very influential part when he was Secretary of Labor. Mr. John Foster Dulles, as Secretary of State, played a very important part. John B. Connally is apparently playing a very important part as Secretary of the Treasury. In brief, we should look more to men than we do to departments for effective leadership. Actually, if you get too big you don't do anything! It seems to me that we would be better off sometimes if we increased the number of agencies and put the responsibilities on them and then have an organization of the White House that sees to it that these organizations effectively operate. In brief, I am no advocate of super departments!

Moreover, it seems to me there is not enough communication between the Congress and the White House staff, and I'm glad that the students have set this problem as the focus for their symposium here under this Center's sponsorship next March. This coordination business should be three way, i.e. between the agency, the White House, and the Congress. I'm for improving agency communication both with the White House and the Congress. And this may require some Congressional committee overhaul as well as some changes in White House organization. But again I emphasize men more than organization—and a desire of the men involved, legislative, executive, and agency, to effectively coordinate. The history of this relationship has been more effective relationship between the agencies and the Congress. This is the old story of being concerned about the hand that feeds them. It seems to me that we especially need more effective agency relationship with the White House and also Congress with the White House.

Finally, the question that I have, is in connection with this recent wage-price freeze: It seemed that there was an example in which there was not very much coordination or much bringing together. It seems to me that the Cost of Living Council itself is not nearly so effective as is the person of John B. Connally. Mr. Connally exercises that leadership through the Council of

Economic Advisers as well as the Treasury and the Wage-Price Board. Yet that Council of Economic Advisers was a particularly effective instrument under President Kennedy, again because of men like Clement Gordon and Walter Heller. So again we come to the human equation. Mr. W. Clement Stone may really have had a point in his keynote emphasis on that point.

So here again you have an example of an agency that is effective because of personal leadership. But why was the Internal Revenue Service selected as the administrative agency? Was it because it has muscle? Otherwise would not a vehicle of the Department of Commerce have been more appropriate?

THOMAS EVANS: Thank you for those examples regarding leadership. Dwight Ink, what happened at the 7:30 meeting when you came to consider the wage-price freeze?

DWIGHT INK: The 7:30 meeting was not the place this was formulated. Camp David happened to be the site of the key formulation of this policy. Dr. Paul W. McCracken, Chairman of the Council of Economic Advisers, played a very key role in that I might say. He and George P. Shultz and Connally and Dr. Arthur F. Burns all played very, very major roles.

One of the reasons that the IRS was selected as the means for carrying this out is because it has a field capacity. It has offices all over the country, while Commerce does not. And part of that decision on the selection of the IRS was that there needed to be a vehicle that was in place and the IRS had one.

You mentioned the staff-Congressional relations. I think this is an area where there could probably be improvement. But I would point out that it is impossible for a man like Ehrlichman to be as accessible to Congressmen as someone in a Department who is concerned with only one area. Mr. Ehrlichman is concerned with the whole domestic area. If he is too readily available to the 100 senators and the 435 Congressmen, he will not have any time to serve the President, and that really is his primary job.

One final comment with respect to more agencies: the problem is that the more agencies you get, the more these program areas become fragments. The more they are fragmented the more the decision-making has to float up to the White House level for decision-making. Since you cannot weight the President with all these kinds of decisions, it means that the White House staff, the OMB staff, are making those decisions. This is what has been referred to as the anonymous group, the most removed from reality in many instances! Certainly creating more agencies greatly stretches out and lengthens and makes more complex the decision-making process and diffuses the responsibility and accountability.

THOMAS EVANS: Since we have time for only one more question and since this is the final session of this, our Second National Leadership Symposium, I am going to call on our host, the chief executive officer of the Center for the Study of the Presidency.

GORDON HOXIE: Thank you, Tom. It is not my desire to preempt the final remarks. However, I appreciate the invitation to make a summary comment and then ask a question.

In our discussions beginning Friday evening, we have sought, primarily by historical analysis, to project a view of the Presidency of the 1970's. We have viewed those forces which rather steadily since 1931 have increased centralization of executive authority.

There were two rather major efforts to decrease the federal bureaucracy over this 40 year period. These were led by former President Hoover, who, reluctantly in his own Administration had, in efforts to combat the depression, begun with the Reconstruction Finance Corporation and other agencies to set this growth by Government in Washington in motion. It was the first and second Hoover Commission of the late 1940's and the mid 1950's that had sought, partially successfully for the time, to arrest this growth.

Now we see emerging what the present President so well describes as a New Federalism, with an effort to redistribute functions and a degree of decision-making down to the state and local levels. Since he who controls the purse controls the power, this will also be accompanied by a new concept of revenue sharing. This perhaps even more than organizational change, should help establish a more balanced relationship between national and state and local authority.

Related to all of this we have also seen not only the proposals for Cabinet reorganization but also proposals to get some of this centralized decision-making and functioning, out of the White House and back into the Cabinet departments.

We have noted that much of this reform came from the Ash Council memoranda of May and November 1970. In his letter of February 5, 1971, releasing the Ash Council report, the President made clear that the specific legislation he was going to recommend would have some variations from the Ash Council report. As the President stated, "The differences will reflect conclusions I have reached as a result of my own experience in government, as well as proposals for executive reorganization made earlier in this Administration and in previous administrations."

These differences included the reorganization of the Department of Transportation which was not a part of the Ash Council Report. The President, with his extremely able Secretary of Transportation, John A. Volpe, reached these conclusions.

Specific reforms in field services, while pointed up by the Ash Council, as they have been pointed up today, again more directly reflected the President's and individual Cabinet member's views.

Many of these new concepts were set forth in the President's message to Congress of March 25, 1971. It is well worth highlighting this message. And in these concluding remarks I would like to quote from it. The President reiterated his observation from his State of the Union Message that "most Americans today are simply fed up with government at all levels. . . ." This, as you know, was a premise that led to the founding of this Center.

In his March 25th message the President placed his reorganizational proposals at the heart of what he termed "a new American Revolution." He suggested that at no time since the Constitutional Convention of 1787 was there need of such concern for reorganization—Congressional and legislative, as well as executive. What he posed is: "what the Federal Government of this Nation ought to look like in the last third of the twentieth century." And he posed the challenge in the words of Alexander Hamilton in the Constitutional debates of 1788 "whether societies of men are really capable or not of establishing good government from reflection and choice. . . ."

My final question then, primarily to Jim Finch and/or Dwight Ink, is, what are the prospects not only for carrying into being the remaining organizational reforms but also this spirit of a "new American Revolution" or a "New Federalism," if you will? Will these become principles of the Presidency, and of the nation in the 1970's, or will they merely be the eloquent expressions of the present President?

JAMES FINCH: I do believe that the President's State of the Union and March 25th messages, to which you refer, have had a very real influence on both the Senate and the House Government Operations Committees. For example, they have deeply influenced Chairman Chet Holifield of the House Committee.

Holifield is a veteran of organizational proposals, having served in the Congress for three decades and having been directly concerned as a member or chairman of the Government Operations Committee. He has heard other messages for reform. But the comprehensiveness of this one and the need have, it is fair to say, caused him to make a 180 degree turn. Like the President, he realized the political pitfalls.

Pitted against such men of vision are the organized interest groups to which Dr. Lyon has referred. These are the people who feel they have a vested interest in maintaining the *status quo*. They are well financed. They are well organized. It will be quite a battle.

One of the keys to success will be getting the debate, the considerations, the discussions, out in the open. In the past Government reorganization has always been considered a colorless, or if, I may use the word, a "sexless" issue. It is not one you can normally get a grass roots uprising in support of. In the past, reorganization has been considered by those in the Congress and in the White House as an in-house issue. That type of view of reorganization makes it very easy for the pressure groups, the people who want to maintain the *status quo*, to remain in the saddle.

But this President is making an effort to carry his messages to the people. He is making an effort to build up public support for the concept of major reform.

This citizens' committee, headed by James M. Roche, who expressed an especial interest to Dr. Hoxie in what you are doing here, is a part of this effort. Given this effort, when it comes down to voting time, be it in 1972, or after the election in 1973, Congressmen will have to give serious consideration before or if they register opposition. They will have to answer the question why they are opposed to progress and reform.

The key then is getting the matter out in the open, having people concerned, considering reorganization and also this spiritual concept of a New Federalism on its merits. Given this effort, I am optimistic.

DWIGHT INK: I agree with the concepts Dr. Hoxie and Mr. Finch have set forth. This is vitally important, and the American people must understand this. My own effort includes assigning my deputy, about two thirds of his time, to this reorganization program. We are putting a great deal of effort forward now.

The prospects before the 1972 elections do remain doubtful. But this President will, if given a mandate in the election, make the program enactment central, I believe, in his second Administration. So I see this as, indeed, characterizing the Presidency of the 1970's. So far as specifics are concerned, the best prospects for enactment are with Community Development and Natural Resources. Human Resources and Economic Affairs remain on the horizon, but they will take tremendous effort and a deal of time before enactment.

HARVEY MANSFIELD: I don't know any reason to disagree with that prognosis. I heard Herbert Roback, who is Congressman Holifield's staff director on Government Operations, speaking about these forthcoming hearings last week. He was not committing himself to an outcome. He was saying that they deserved to be heard, and they would be heard. It was also plain that the opposition groups had not yet surfaced. The extent and intensity of their efforts really cannot be judged at this time. I believe I would agree with the Finch-Hoxie-Ink appraisal.

THOMAS EVANS: In concluding, may I express our appreciation again to Dr. Hoxie and his staff for a most productive symposium.

By way of a brief concluding remark, may I again recall the observation of the late John F. Kennedy. He was asked in a press conference whether McGeorge Bundy and the National Security Council were arrogating to themselves too much power. His reply: "I shall continue to exercise some residual authority."

The point is that the President's organization, the organization of the Executive Office, traditionally does reflect the style, the personality, of the President. This hearkens back to the succinct keynote remarks of W. Clement Stone, who is a keen observer of human nature and a close personal friend of this President.

Last year, in our symposium here, Tommy Corcoran characterized the New Deal as the period of disorderly genius. Roosevelt did reach out for one man and then another and another. Some of them were specialists and some of them were generalists. Many of them were endowed with political background; many were not. But most, like Roosevelt himself, were endowed with political sensitivity. This was his method of doing things.

It has been frequently suggested, often by members of the academic community, that the President should be insulated against the highly persuasive personalities who surround him, who are close to him or next to him. And yet ironically when there is a John Kenneth Galbraith or an Arthur M. Schlesinger, Jr. they seem to have a lesser concern about such influences.

George Reedy has taken a somewhat different tact. In this symposium last year and again this year, based upon his own observation of the 1960's, he warned against insulating the President from reality. You remember his book *Twilight of the Presidency* was introduced here.

So far as the 70's are concerned Dr. Hoxie suggested that the angle of the sun was the same at dawn as at twilight and perhaps this reorganization in spirit as well as structure will contribute to a rising rather than a setting sun in the 1970's. I am inclined to agree with that more optimistic view.

Tommy Corcoran added last year that "we welcome having the Republicans occasionally to tidy the joint up." Walter Thayer with equal charm responded as a member of the Ash Council, that that was what they were about. But he added that it was more than just a tidying up, it was a major overhaul and a change of philosophy. This is what I perceive as the Presidency of the 1970's.

This President is a man who likes organization not for organization's sake but for goal accomplishment. This President does not seek a system of disorderly genius. I have had the pleasure of working with him quite closely both in legal matters and in political matters. He does like to have a staff which can give him a series of alternatives from which he can make his decision. But more than that he sees this as a crossroads, a new sense of national direction, as we approach the nation's bicentennial. In that spirit the chair exercises the prerogative of closing, on a non-partisan note, in support of the Ash Council's, the President's recommendations. These can profoundly shape the Presidency of the 1970's and beyond.

GORDON HOXIE: Thank you, Tom Evans, and thank you all for your outstanding contributions. If I may be so bold, concerned Americans will find interest in the record of these proceedings. In this I respectfully include the President.

The National Leadership Symposium stands adjourned.

CHAPTER VI

Summing Up: A Resumé
by R. Gordon Hoxie

THE KEYNOTE: HUMANIZING THE PRESIDENCY

As a part of a triple keynote, W. Clement Stone, the Center's Honorary Chairman, emphasized the personal aspect of the Presidency and the importance of humanizing the office, "for when we deal with the progress, problems and activities of a nation, we are dealing with people."

On a similar note, Press Secretary to President Johnson, George E. Reedy, Jr. noted, "Our problem is not keeping power away from the President, but finding some way of humanizing this...", the world's most powerful lay office. In proportion to the increasing complexity of the office, Mr. Reedy believes it has been the more removed from the people. It was further, Reedy believes, this sense of removal in the decade of the 60's which brought the Presidency "to its sharpest challenge."

In reality, "there is no power whatsoever in any political office." The Presidency is rather an "instrument through which political power can be exercised." Mr. Reedy contends that "President Kennedy . . . was definitely losing his political force at the time he made his trip to Dallas." In retrospect he views President Eisenhower as "a master politician. I did not think so at the time," he concludes, "I was a typical partisan Democrat. . . . Lord, it is funny how different things look a few years later."

In a similar view, Mr. Eisenhower's Press Secretary, James C. Hagerty, noted that "Mr. Eisenhower . . . had one basic understanding that is fundamental in politics. He had mastered the art of compromise, of achieving the common good without the surrender of principle and integrity."

Mr. Hagerty emphasized that the Presidency must be viewed in terms of the times, the 50's were far different than the 60's. "It was an entirely different world and an entirely different ballgame."

Mr. Eisenhower was not certain how objectively either his own Presidency or that of Mr. Johnson was viewed. He wrote Mr. Hagerty on October 18, 1966 ". . . words rather than . . . achievement . . . are taken by columnists and partisans, and at times, by serious students, as evidence of the true capacities of those of whom they write." He found that too often achievement was equated "with the exaggerated use of the vertical pronoun."

Again emphasizing the human qualities, Mr. Hagerty concluded that a great President must "be a man of great wisdom and great patience. . . ."

Both Mr. Hagerty and Mr. Reedy had come to the Symposium from testifying on Capitol Hill their opposition to Senator Birch Bayh's proposal for a constitutional amendment for a one-term, six-year Presidency. While opposing the amendment they were concerned lest we be headed in the direction of single-term Presidents. Such they conceived as reflecting the climate of the times, an absence of consensus, of belief in a set of principles, in an ideal, a goal. There is more than personal charisma in getting people to want to "saddle up and ride to Jerusalem." The present President is seeking to build a consensus around a "new majority." It remains to be seen whether that can be accomplished. If it can, the effectiveness of the Presidential office will again be enhanced.

SECURITY, DIPLOMACY, FREEDOM OF INFORMATION, AND SCHOLARSHIP

These four phrases are interrelated in our society, and considerable confusion relates to them. Former Librarian of Congress Luther H. Evans, notes that "a lot of people have not drawn a clear enough distinction between freedom of access and freedom to print." Dr. Evans points out that when the First Amendment referred to freedom of the press that "it meant that if you had access you had freedom to print, but it had nothing to do . . . with the right of access." Thus, he concludes, "Here the *New York Times* may have been a little bit wrong in the case of the Pentagon Papers. They did not get the right to print . . . because they did not have the legal right to access."

In a similar vein Martin S. Hayden, Editor-in-Chief, *Detroit News*, suggests that if James Reston had gone to President Nixon and sought such permission for the *Times* to print the Pentagon Papers, it would probably have been granted. Himself a former Washington correspondent, Hayden concluded that "very few things that are secret stay secret in Washington indefinitely."

Hayden and former Presidential Press Secretaries Reedy and Hagerty noted that the publication of the Pentagon Papers had not caused a great stir because of the attitude towards the Vietnam War, where as Reedy expressed it, "people thought they had been sold a bill of goods. . . . " However, a disclosure which might outrage the Congress and the people could result in a suppressive secrecy act.

Like Dr. Evans, Reedy, Hagerty, and Hayden deplored overclassification. Dr. Evans recalled his own discussions with Mr. Eisenhower on the subject, the latter encouraging him to "keep working at it."

The Nixon Administration has made progress on the subject, breathing new life into the 1966 Freedom of Information Act. Additionally, subsequent to this Symposium, in March 1972, Mr. Nixon ordered the first major overhaul in two decades in the system of protecting diplomatic and military classified matters. Concerning this subject President Nixon stated: "Fundamental to our way of life is the belief that, when information which properly belongs to the public is systematically withheld by those in power, the people become ignorant of their own affairs, distrustful of those who manage them, and eventually—incapable of determining their own destinies."

Dr. Robert H. Connery, Professor of Political Science, Columbia University and President of the Academy of Political Science, declared "in terms of the amount of information available to the American people . . ., I would evaluate our whole structure of government as far in advance of most, if not all, governments in the world. . . ."

There was general consensus that the Americans are the best informed public, so informed *both* by the government and the media. "What worries me," Hayden declared, "is this constant battle between the press and the bureaucracy to get information out." Competition between the government and the media is healthy so long as there is mutual respect. Where that departs, comes repression.

Dr. William M. Franklin, Director, Historical Office, U.S. Department of State, attested that, "In comparison with foreign offices of other nations, our publication in the field of foreign relations is the most and the longest. Indeed," he added, "it is fully comparable to the Pentagon Papers in everything but time."

177

Related to Dr. Franklin's observations, Dr. Harvey Branscomb, Chancellor Emeritus, Vanderbilt University, suggested "more use . . . of the so-called 'White Paper'. . . . It would be of enormous help toward the understanding of the national course and in charting and delineating the national debate."

Describing policy-making as necessarily "an elite function," Dr. H. Coleman McGinnis of the University of Tennessee underscored the importance "of a full flow of information and debate within the halls of government." George Reedy went beyond this in a plea for a national debate, as a safety valve letting "people blow off steam, no matter how unreasonably and how unreasoned. . . ." By his view the President would be more attentive to such varying views outside than he would within Government where "he is one of the few men in the world who can really create his own environment."

Taking issue with Reedy's concept that the President listened only to one voice, one he wanted to hear, Major General Robert N. Ginsburgh, Chief, Office of Air Force History, contended that President Johnson, whom he had served as an aide, had tried to listen to too many voices.

While agreeing with Reedy that "any President is isolated," John Roy Price, Jr., Special Assistant to President Nixon, emphasized that this President "does insist before any major decision is made . . . upon having it clearly stated . . . where his people stand. . . . This," Price concluded, ". . . is . . . different from what has gone on before."

DOMESTIC POLICY FOR THE 1970's

Dr. Connery perceived that "domestic problems, and in the area of domestic problems, urban problems, are the major ones for the 70's; problems of mass transportation, education, health, housing, and control of capital."

Special Assistant to the President John Price announced, ". . . the New Deal is dead. . . . What we will see emerging over the next decade is . . . a response by our people to the growing recognition that the central government cannot . . . solve every problem. . . ." In picturesque language Price referred to the "arthritis" or the unresponsiveness of government. He expounded his "Barnacle Theory of the Federal Government"—one Government program encrusted upon another, and hard to scrape off. He explained the lack of enthusiasm to come to the Federal

Government for aid on the part of state and local government officials. They must feel "a little bit like you are under water looking up at a Portuguese man-of-war with thousands of tentacles hanging down towards you. Needless to say," Price concludes in this image that Daniel Patrick Moynihan had suggested, "you are not sure that you want to grab any one of them."

James M. Beggs, Under Secretary of Transportation, deplored the red tape in getting through the multiple layers of government. Hence he advocated as necessary the New Federalism and revenue sharing, letting state and local communities make more of their own decisions. "This flexibility," Beggs concluded "is absolutely essential . . . so that they can . . . solve problems as they see them." Additionally, Beggs perceived a structural problem for state and local jurisdictions in working with multiple-jurisdiction agencies, ranging from a small water district to the giant Port of New York Authority. Certain consolidations in local government may be in order.

In like spirit, Ray B. Chambers, Deputy Assistant Secretary, HEW, avowed, "just as Franklin Roosevelt began the New Deal, . . . Richard Nixon is beginning a new trend in government that will not be reversed—regardless of administration." It is Chambers' assessment that ". . . while . . . there may be some wheel-spinning in the first years of this Administration, I do believe we are moving decision-making slowly but surely, if haltingly, out to the local units of government."

Dr. Connery added approvingly, "I like . . . Mr. Nixon's concept, to evolve power and evolve control at the lowest possible level in order to free government and particularly the Federal Government to deal with the more important aspects of life."

William, J. Casey, Chairman of the Securities and Exchange Commission, would go beyond the redistribution of "power and control" to state and local units. He would further distribute to the private sector responsibilities currently in the public sphere. ". . . we have giantism throughout our governmental structure," Casey declared. "That giantism is going to have to be broken down; there are going to have to be more partnerships between the public sector and the private sector."

Although sharing Mr. Casey's hopes for a redistribution between the private and public sectors, Robert A. Podesta, Assistant Secretary of Commerce, was doubtful of this being brought about unless we "have another American Revolution. So we ought to quit talking about the welfare state; it is here; and we have got it. What we are trying to do here," Podesta concluded, "is manage it better. And that is very unromantic, from a political standpoint."

For Mr. Chambers, participation is the key. He agrees, for example, that HEW programs have helped make us healthier. For him the real question is, "How do we make it possible for all Americans to buy in?"

Mr. Casey examined our economic goals and concluded "we are going to have to double the rate at which public savings are mobilized and brought into capital uses to meet economic needs over the decade of the 1970's." Moreover, he related our vigor of health in the international economy to that at home.

Although organization was the topic of the final round table, inevitably it entered into the discussions regarding both domestic and foreign policy. Beyond organization there is the matter of goals. Under Secretary Beggs suggested they need fuller defining, also study as to their effects at the secondary and tertiary levels. Related thereto Mr. Beggs asserted the need for evaluation, "on the Federal level of determining whether we are performing well, badly, or indifferently." In a plea for Cabinet reorganization, he asserted "we have not yet succeeded in relating our domestic departments to the rather broad authority we have to spend money." Beggs found Congressional reorganization likewise "long overdue."

In a related matter, Mr. Podesta contended that ". . . the least understood activity in the Federal Government is the budget process. In my own estimation," Podesta concluded, "half the Congress does not understand it, and I may be being charitable." Mr. Podesta agreed that "these OMB people and the White House guys" work awfully hard, but he is not certain that "they always read what the President says."

In the matter of what the President says, one of "the White House guys," John Price, admitted that "men like myself . . . fight to be the last one near the mimeograph machine when the stencil is cut the night before the message goes to Congress."

There was general agreement that the President does not enjoy the broad power in domestic policy that he does in foreign policy. About the only example of "raw Presidential power" in the domestic sphere that Mr. Price and Mr. Thomas Evans could bring to mind was the removal, after more than a year's effort, of the "temporary" buildings on the mall, that had been there since World War I.

Although Mr. Price rated the professionalism of the career service people as high, there was general agreement that the execution of Presidential policy left something to be desired. As Mr. Beggs put it ". . . you sort of get to feel that the OMB might not be serving the same President you are serving! Your rationale is that you are serving the public! And poor old OMB hears that from everybody in the Government." In point of fact, Beggs concluded: "one has to continually remind himself, the commissions and departments, that his responsibility first is to the public interest . . . and only secondly to the constituency."

C. Edwin Gilmour, Professor of Political Science at Grinnell College, described this thwarting of the public interest. Much of it is to be blamed on the relationships between special interest groups and committees of the Congress. As an example of these so-called "policy cluster groups" he cited the relationships between the Farm Bureau Federation and the House and Senate Agricultural committees. Such a " 'policy cluster' . . . is beyond the control of the President; it is beyond the control of the Congress and . . . beyond the control of the public. Here then," Dr. Gilmour concluded, "is power that is irresponsible."

Dr. Mary S. Calderone, director Sex Information Education Council U.S., concluded with a plea for the participation of the social or soft scientists in policy formulation as compared to the imput by the pure or hard scientists. Mr. Beggs agreed that ". . . we do need a structure of government that makes available to the Presidency and the Congress equally the new findings in the social sciences." Mr. Price called attention to this Administration's innovations in this area, as the result of an interdepartmental committee set up by Dr. Moynihan.

Dr. Connery asserted in response to criticisms of our system in general and lack of planning in particular that "we are beginning to plan for the future. But planning has to be based upon some evaluation of the past." In terms of freedom and information as government goals he evaluated our system "as far in advance of most, if not all, governments in the world. . . . If Communism fails," he added, "as it in my mind has, it is because of an overloading in the system, putting too much control into the government and too many decisions to be made by it."

FOREIGN POLICY FOR THE 70's

Chairman Casey stated that "today . . . increasingly the Congress is seeking to exercise control in foreign policy, control which it had wrested from President Wilson, only to have it taken back by President F. D. Roosevelt." In describing the "Nixon Doctrine", he asserted "we have come a long way since John Kennedy said in 1961 that we were prepared to pay any price and bear any burden to maintain freedom throughout the world. We have come to believe through the experience of the last ten years, and this is a view shared by public opinion in the United States, that our power does not reach as far as we thought it did. We have come to believe that it is not as important as we thought it was to know all and control all in all parts of the globe."

In describing the Nixon Doctrine Chairman Casey compared it to "maintaining a global balance on somewhat the same basis that England maintained a European balance for three centuries."

The Nixon Doctrine divests ourselves of the role as the world's policeman, a role we never had prior to the end of World War II. "Our interests," it states, "must shape our commitments, rather than the other way around." Secondly, it states that if a nuclear power threatens the freedom of our allies or "of a nation whose survival we consider vital to our security", we shall provide a shield. Our allies and such nations are not asked to participate in nuclear armament, quite the contrary. Thirdly, in case of non-nuclear aggression we shall again assume our treaty obligations, including economic and military assistance. However, the primary responsibility for manpower for defense shall be on the part of the threatened nation.

It is in keeping with the Nixon Doctrine that with allies like South Vietnam and South Korea our troop withdrawals have been accompanied by upgrading those countries' equipment, supplies, and training.

Within the Nixon Doctrine there have developed special corollaries as related to China and the Soviet Union. As Chairman Casey suggests, ". . . the President has decided that the time has come to deal with the reality of 800 million Chinese on the Asiatic mainland." At the same time ". . . the question of the strategic balance between the United States and the Soviet Union is a matter ... of enormous continuing concern to the Presidency." Chairman Casey points out that *vis à vis* the Soviet Union as superiority becomes parity, should it become inferiority, we might find ourselves in a situation not unlike the Soviet Union did when it had to step down in the 1962 crisis.

In this regard Lt. General Glen W. Martin, Vice Commander in Chief, SAC, reaffirmed that "the most vital *security issue* of the Seventies is the relationship between the strategic power of the United States and that of the Soviet Union."

Mr. Richard A. Ware, former Principal Deputy Assistant Secretary of Defense for International Security Affairs, further traced policy changes. "There has been ... under President Nixon, an historic change in United States foreign policy, perhaps the first major change since the days of Woodrow Wilson."

Where Chairman Casey traced the Nixon Doctrine as related to China and Soviet Union policy, Mr. Ware gave particular attention to Great Britain and Japan. He noted historically the special relationships with the United Kingdom. "Today, with an insurgency within its own border in Northern Ireland, one may well ask whether the United States can depend upon the United Kingdom in the future, over the next 25 years, as the keystone or linchpin to our relationship to the defense of Europe."

The problem with Japan is different. It is, in reality, "... the question as to whether or not Japan for evermore can be considered a friend and ally of the United States. After all," Mr. Ware concluded, "twice in a century it reversed course 180°."

Mr. Ware also emphasized the pressures upon us to withdraw our troops both from the Far East and Europe. In the latter, with the end of the Vietnam War, the pressure will increase. Lack of Congressional support, inbred opposition in the Congress, such as has been witnessed with foreign aid, raises the spector of decline in our credibility image. This suggests the great dilemma of the 70's: "Can a major power, such as the United States, stand down and still continue to exert world-wide influence, especially when other countries know that the South Vietnamese experience has soured the taste of the U.S. population for overseas military involvement?"

Where economic and military power had been principal considerations in structuring foreign policy, according to Mr. Frank J. Shakespeare, Jr. of the USIA, a new dimension has been added in the impact of television at the dining table, in the living room and the bedroom. Mr. Ware concludes that "If our foreign policy were ever determined by a political or leadership elite, I would submit I do not think it is true any longer."

The advantages and perils of summit diplomacy were discussed. Dean Acheson was quoted as saying that "when a chief of state, or head of government, makes a fumble in a direct negotiation with another head of state, the goal line is open behind him."

Helmut Sonnenfeldt, Senior Staff Member, National Security Council, assures us ". . . this President was perhaps as cautious about that particular device of diplomacy . . . as any of his predecessors." He found Mr. Nixon cognizant and mindful of the problems in this regard that had been experienced by Presidents Eisenhower, Kennedy, and Johnson.

To the suggestion taken from a book by Herbert Hoover on President Wilson (the only book by a President about another President) that the mystique of office is removed by the actual presence of the President, Mr. Sonnenfeldt had a ready reply: ". . . the people of Peking and the people of Moscow will not have lived until they have seen the Presidential entourage arrive in Peking and Moscow."

What did concern Mr. Sonnenfeldt, were American attitudes *vis à vis* foreign policy. "Whereas in the earlier period, we had thought ourselves too good to be a part of the world, many of our people came to . . . think us too bad to be a part of the world." He concluded, "that a President can no longer, . . . at least in the early 1970's, count on the idealism and devotion that made American involvement possible in the previous periods."

Although pointing out that "we do have serious problems at home," Mr. Sonnenfeldt contended that "we would make a mistake if we . . . assume . . . that in the Communist world, there are not divergencies, differences, fissures. . . ."

Despite his high motivation to focus on the ending of the war in Vietnam, President Johnson's renunciation in 1968 of his right to run again "does not," in Mr. Sonnenfeldt's estimation, "enhance the power of the Presidency." He contends that ". . . whatever the precise balance between the President and the Congress . . . this system of government depends upon a strong and vigorous Presidency."

Several of the participants related effective foreign and domestic policy. Major General Robert N. Ginsburgh, Chief, Office of Air Force History, emphasized that ". . . if the U.S. is to achieve its current domestic objectives, President Nixon will have to preserve adequate military force as this war in Vietnam draws to a close and thereafter." In his estimation, ". . . the Nixon-Kissinger team has substantially achieved the objectives for which we entered the war in Vietnam. . . ."

In a discussion of the adequacy of force levels, General Ginsburgh mentioned as among the determinants, in both short and long range: "the outcome of such things as: the President's trip to Peking . . .; the President's trip to Moscow; the result of the SALT talks . . .; the . . . result of President Nixon's new economic programs; the result of MBFR . . .; plus the true intentions and the capabilities of our political adversaries." He suggested we were more properly *coping* with rather than *solving* problems in the foreign relations sphere and that in this sphere the challenges in international economics would be the most difficult.

Several of the speakers addressed the issue of Presidential-Congressional relations in the foreign policy sphere. Proposals such as Senator Javits' war powers bill were discussed. The solution was not found, however, in institutional, in legal, changes, though "certain internal reforms within the Congress" were suggested by General Ginsburgh. Although this editor suggested "the solution . . . cannot be legislated," Mr. Grimes was so specific as to state that ". . . the Javits proposal is not going to force the kind of consultation message to create a new consensus. On the contrary," Grimes concluded, "it will institutionalize the problem."

The growing and cumbersome machinery in national security policy was a matter of concern. It was pointed out, to the surprise of some, that many agencies today involved in national security policy are larger than the State Department, including both the CIA and AID. Even the USIA is about 30% the size of the State Department. There are more Defense than State Department representatives in the U.S. embassies. The growth of this "little foreign office" in the Defense Department, at the Pentagon (Office of the Assistant Secretary for International Security Affairs) has found a response over in Foggy Bottom in the

Office of the Director of Politico-Military Affairs. In brief, layer upon layer has been built in national security policy machinery, machinery which must be pared down for the effective execution of national security policy in the 1970's.

Finally, it was the Director, Historical Office, Department of State, who asked the most haunting question about the national will: "What brought about this loss of prestige? What brought our travail of the 60's?" Dr. Franklin believes if we can regain something of our idealism, our sense of national purpose and will, then in the 1970's and only then, "less force would be necessary for American leadership to be effective throughout the world."

ORGANIZATION FOR THE 1970's

Although concerns for organization of the Executive Branch, its relationships with the Legislative and with state and local authority, appeared throughout the Symposium, the final focus was on organization, gearing up for the 70's and beyond. This concluding session was largely built about the President's views on organization and the recommendations of the President's Advisory Council on Executive Organization (i.e. the Ash Council).

The President began with his now famous premise that "most Americans today are simply fed up with government at all levels. . . ." (As this editor noted, "this . . . was a premise that led to the founding of this Center.") Beyond this the President's challenge for what he termed "a new American Revolution" of federal, state, and local relationships, was "what the Federal Government of this nation ought to look like in the last third of the twentieth century." He hearkened back to the challenge expressed by Alexander Hamilton in the debates of 1788 over the adoption of the Federal Constitution: "whether societies of men are really capable or not of establishing good government from reflection and choice."

Basic in the President's philosophy is what he terms a New Federalism, a redistribution of authority and responsibility from the Federal to the state and local levels. This he envisions as being accomplished in part by revenue sharing and in part by eliminating the confusing overlapping of Federal agencies working with state and local communities.

Turning to the Ash Council the President in essence asked how to "best organize the Executive Branch of Government to operate more efficiently. . . ." In response Mr. Ash had a hard look at the diffused and overlapping areas of responsibility in the Federal Establishment. As James H. Finch, Jr., Executive Director of the Citizens Committee for Government Reorganization expressed it, "Roy Ash said from time to time . . . that when many people are responsible no one is responsible."

Specifically, they had recommended the creation of the Domestic Council, paralleling in the domestic field the National Security Council in the foreign policy area. It had been the hope that the result would be the upgrading of the Cabinet Departments concerned in domestic affairs as well as their more effective coordination. Mr. John D. Ehrlichman, Assistant to the President for Domestic Affairs, had been named Director of the Council, created in 1970. By the time of this Symposium it could be said that much of the hope for the Domestic Council was being realized.

Also in 1970, the recommendation of the Ash group for reorganizing the Office of the Budget as the Office of Management and Budget had been effectively accomplished.

The Ash Council moved on then to a major restructuring of the Cabinet Departments along the lines of the major domestic purposes of government. Thus they conceived of four super Cabinet Departments that would replace seven existing Departments (Agriculture, Commerce, HEW, HUD, Interior, Labor, and Transportation) plus several other agencies. These new "Super Departments" would be Community Development, Economic Affairs, Human Resources, and Natural Resouces. (The Post Office Department had in 1971 become an independent government corporation, the U.S. Postal Service. And the other departments in domestic affairs, Treasury and Justice, would remain intact).

Mr. Finch, who had been executive director of the Ash Council, emphasized that "it was not preconceptions but rather the *experiences* as we worked our way through the study that led to those proposals for overall Cabinet reorganization and consolidations."

In some pithy observations, while sometimes serving as the devil's advocate, Dr. Harvey C. Mansfield, Professor of Political

Science at Columbia University, asked several searching questions and made several cogent observations. Dr. Mansfield, who had worked on the most sweeping prior changes in the Executive Office, those affected by the Brownlow Commission of 1936, observed that "there can be a good many reasons for organization or reorganization, some of them cynical, some of them personal to appointees. . . . But a proposal of this sort, for broad super departments seems to have as its main rationale the improvement of coordination of activities that are divided or shared among a great many federal agencies."

John A. Wells, the senior partner of the firm of Royall, Koegel, and Wells, observed that in Mr. Hoover's time the Executive Branch was like a pyramid, with the President on top and immediately below him the Cabinet Departments. Such is no longer the case. Today the organization is like a wheel, with the hub the President; immediately about him are such key assistants as Mr. Ehrlichman in Domestic Affairs, Dr. Kissinger in National Security Affairs, and Mr. H. R. Haldeman, Administrative Affairs.

Supporting this new concept, Mr. Wells concluded, "When it gets over to the Executive, power cannot be dispersed. It has to be centralized and rationalized and made internally consistent." This concept does raise the question of access both to the President and to those key assistants. Mr. Dwight A. Ink, Jr., Assistant Director, OMB, speculated "I suppose there are occasions in which some Cabinet members feel they are going through Mr. Ehrlichman, when they feel they ought to be going directly to the President."

On the other side of the coin, access of Congress to these key assistants, Mr. Ink asserted that "Mr. Ehrlichman is concerned with the whole domestic area. If he is too readily available to the 100 senators and the 435 Congressmen, he will not have any time to serve the President, and that really is his primary job."

Although part of the reorganization philosophy is to prevent trivia from coming up to the President, in no way can or should any President be precluded from any major policy matters except for reasons of health or other inability to hold office. Moreover, as Mr. Sonnenfeldt expressed it, "There is no way in which Presidential prestige and influence can be transferred to a subordinate agency. . . . On a closely contested issue," Sonnenfeldt concluded, "only the Presidency has the prestige and the clout to put it over." It is only the President who can create "the kind of political consensus which has to be built around a decision." Perhaps more than any other President since Lincoln, this President insists, after getting all of the staff views, in making his own decisions. It was Mr. Lincoln, who on an issue in which he had strong convictions, said the "Ayes have it", when all of his Cabinet member voted "Nay."

No organizational changes will completely eliminate the "sort of natural tension", as Mr. Sonnenfeldt expressed it, between a new President and career personnel who sometimes "tend to see these periodic arrivals in the White House as some intruders into their own guardianship of the national interest." Nonetheless Mr. Grimes emphasized for effective policy implementation the bureaucracy must believe in the policy *and* believe that the President does. Mr. Grimes, Deputy Under Secretary of the Navy, was impressed by and read the observation of Mr. Sonnenfeldt made at this Center's first Montauk Symposium: ". . . a President is [not] a great President only if he makes wise decisions. He becomes truly a great President only after he has succeeded in enforcing those decisions."

Finally, the Symposium members turned their attention to the prospects of carrying out the balance of these reorganization proposals, those built about the Cabinet reorganization, requiring Congressional approval. Short of that the Symposium members predicted that the President might designate certain of these Cabinet members as counsellors or assistants, thereby bringing them into the focal point of power in coordinating roles approaching the scope of the would-be heads of the four "super departments." [This is precisely what has occurred in the first days of the second Nixon Administration.]

In mounting an effective campaign for enactment of the President's proposals, all agree with Mr. Finch that vital "to success will be getting the debate, the considerations, the discussions out in the open." Mr. Finch noted that "in the past Government reorganization has always been considered a . . . sexless issue. . . . [It] has been considered by those in the Congress and in the White House as an in-house issue. That type of view of reorganization makes it very easy for the pressure groups, the people who want to maintain the *status quo,* to remain in the saddle."

Dr. Mansfield agreed. He pointed to an earlier reorganization attempt in which the ground work for support had not been laid. This was the proposal of President Johnson to consolidate the Departments of Commerce and Labor. As George Reedy noted, it failed due to labor's opposition. Dr. Mansfield cautioned that for success, reorganization must recognize the positions of "the battalions of political power."

Little hope was realistically held out for securing support for Cabinet reorganization prior to the 1972 Presidential election. It was predicted that if strongly re-elected the President would make his election victory a mandate for carrying this program into effect, that this President would then make a concerted effort to carry his message to the people.

The round table chairman, Thomas W. Evans, a partner in the law firm in which the President had been a member, made a moving peroration for support: "This President is a man who likes organization not for organization's sake but for goal accomplishment." Alluding to the New Deal, Mr. Evans asserted, "This President does not seek a system of disorderly genius. . . . He sees this as a crossroads, a new sense of national direction, as we approach the nation's bi-centennial."

And so this second Montauk Symposium drew to a close. Only time would tell whether this President's conceptions of a new American Revolution in man's relationship with his fellow-man and with his government would be accomplished. What was certain was that this President had given new direction which would characterize the Presidency of the 1970's, and perhaps beyond.

Index